SIR ALEX

SIMPLY THE BEST

HARRY HARRIS

AD LIB

First published in 2021 by Ad Lib Publishers Ltd
15 Church Road
London, SW13 9HE

www.adlibpublishers.com

Text © 2021 Harry Harris

Paperback ISBN 978-1-913543-52-5
eBook ISBN 978-1-913543-50-1

A CIP catalogue record for this book is available from the
British Library.

Every reasonable effort has been made to trace copy-
right-holders of material reproduced in this book, but if
any have been inadvertently overlooked the publishers
would be glad to hear from them.

Printed in the UK

Contents

Foreword

By Bryan Robson

"Fergie screamed at me: 'Get It Sorted!'"

Sir Alex has to be regarded as one of the best, if not the best, club managers in the world. That includes the current best in Jurgen Klopp and Pep Guardiola. Klopp has done really well, but still has a long way to go to match Sir Alex. Guardiola certainly is on his way to matching Sir Alex when you look at what he has won at Barcelona, Bayern Munich and Manchester City. But the big question with Guardiola is whether he will want to keep going to try to achieve as much, if not more, than Sir Alex. With Pep you don't know when he might just opt to retire. There is no knowing with him how long he will want to go on.

With Sir Alex he went on for more than any manager in modern times is likely to want to carry on, and in his time he won a phenomenal amount.

But it is right that you would talk about Sir Alex in the company of Guardiola and Klopp, the two managers currently making such an impact in English football with City and Liverpool and such magnificent teams. Sir Alex's success needs to be judged not just at his phenomenal achievements at United, but what he did at Aberdeen where he did a great job in breaking the dominance of

Celtic and Rangers in winning a European competition with so many young players.

Sir Alex got into the habit of winning titles before he arrived at Old Trafford and once he got his first with United it was a steady stream of silverware. Most impressive was how he built three magnificent teams, all of them having such great success. What he was doing at the club and how he did it didn't surprise me because I was there with him for eight years. I saw at first hand his exceptional skills, his man-management and how his recruitment structure played such a big part in his ability to build those three teams.

A top club will have a lot of money to spend, but invariably, they can waste fortunes if that money is not spent on the right players. But Sir Alex made a habit of spending it wisely, he regularly brought in the right players. Sir Alex had this uncanny knack of replacing one top player with another top player when he needed to, and that was due to the scouting system he put into place. He prioritised a player's background, he only wanted players with really good characters, and stepped up that policy when bringing in strong characters who had their opinions. He was never afraid of that, which was another part of his man-management skills. Another was keeping players happy when leaving them out of the side at times, but that meant often leaving out excellent players.

There was never a better example than the season he won the treble, when he had Ole Gunnar Solskjaer, Andy Cole, Dwight Yorke and Teddy Sheringham to keep happy when he could only play two from four at any given time. He needed all his man-management skills to pull that off. In addition, he was outstanding at bringing young players through just as he had done at Aberdeen. Those ingredients made him the top, top manager.

Sir Alex is also synonymous with the managerial 'hairdryer', and I almost was on the receiving end of it, well, half a hairdryer! We were playing up at Newcastle and it was going badly, we were losing 1–0 and Gazza was running us ragged. We didn't really know much about Gazza back then, but we certainly found out quickly when he was having such a good game against us. I could see what was coming at half time, so I thought it best to get in first. I said, "Yeah we didn't know much about him, but I will try to get it sorted in the second half."

Fergie screamed at me: "Get it sorted!" So I got it sorted in the second half. It was definitely a hairdryer moment, but more half a hairdryer, as I had seen much worse, and you definitely don't want to be on the receiving end of the full hairdryer!

I had seen quite a few of the hairdryer treatments he dished out over the years, and the first one was a confrontation he had with Paul McGrath, but I knew what to expect as we had been tipped off by Gordon Strachan who played for him at Aberdeen, so we were warned.

Fergie used it mostly to test the young players, as he wanted to keep their feet on the ground. But in the latter stages of his career, he didn't find the need to dish out the hairdryer nearly as much; he had calmed down a lot.

I still see quite a bit of 'The Gaffer', we go racing together with some mutual friends, and I see him most times at the games at Old Trafford. I am sure he misses being in the dug-out, you always miss it, playing or managing, but equally I know he is also enjoying his retirement. It is well earned. But he now has more time for his racing, more time for his family, especially now he has so many grandchildren.

Introduction

The Greatest Manager of All Time

Having written books detailing the life and times of great managers from Bill Nicholson to Jose Mourinho, I have no doubt that Sir Alex is the greatest of them all. With a momentous trophy haul and remarkable longevity, the man had an insatiable obsession to be a winner. He emulated the 'Busby Babes' with his own 'Class of '92'. He surpassed his mentor Jock Stein, overtook Sir Matt at Old Trafford, and trumped even the legends of Anfield, Bill Shankly, Bob Paisley, and Kenny Dalglish in the legacy he left after more than a quarter of a century in one of the hottest hot seats in football.

Ferguson famously walked through the doors at Old Trafford declaring that his intent was to knock Liverpool off their f—— perch, and he succeeded. Ferguson now into his 80th year says, "I don't know where that came from. I'm not sure I even said that. But it gathered mileage over the years. Liverpool's success over the 1970s and 1980s was phenomenal and to get to them I had to take a road that was going to be difficult. It meant having to wait in terms of building the club up instead of building a team and eventually it turned out fantastically."

The stats don't lie, and his destiny with winning, manifested in a trophy laden career that takes him right to the top of the managerial all-time listings. Awarded the OBE in 1985 two years after Aberdeen's European Cup Winners' Cup win over Real Madrid, the CBE in the 1995 New Year Honours List for his formidable achievements at United. The knighthood duly arrived after United's phenomenal treble in 1999.

One of the most successful bosses north of the border with eleven trophies at Pittodrie, where he steered Aberdeen to three Premier League titles, four Scottish Cup triumphs, plus the League Cup, Drybrough Cup, European Cup Winners' Cup and European Super Cup was an immense record, especially for a club not part of the Old Firm. At United he delivered an FA Cup Final replay victory over Crystal Palace in 1990 to become the first post-war to manage cup-winning clubs north and south of the border. A year later he regained United's reputation abroad with the European Cup Winners' Cup. In 1992 the League Cup went to Old Trafford for the first time and in 1993 he won the inaugural Premier League. He guided United to the FA Cup and Premiership double in 1994 and repeated the feat two years later as the trophy haul gathered pace.

The first piece of silverware is always the most important, the FA Cup was Sir Alex's turning point, another was ending the club's twenty-six-year wait for a league title, landing the precious first title by ten points from Villa. Sir Alex said, "Oh, the day we won the league for the first time. God Almighty! I couldn't get out of the car park! There were thousands of them. I went there in the afternoon because they wanted a photograph taken with the trophy. There were thousands there and I couldn't get out of my car, they were engulfing me. It was unbelievable. So what you were doing that day was satisfying the anxiety and relief of twenty-six years. These supporters had been suffering for twenty-six years and finally that day they showed their love for me. They could have made me President for that day!"

But those stats tell part of the story of the man and the manager. Fergie was a Jekyll and Hyde, the mood swings were legendary – from smiling, approachable, warm, caring to torrents of abuse. This book goes in search of the real Fergie, the man behind the mask, told by the people who know him best.

The two faces of Fergie are illustrated perfectly in his dealing with two Portuguese wingers, Nani and Ronaldo. Nani relished his dream move to United, but not the nightmare of working under a manager who was "very scary," petrified of doing something wrong. He said: "I was scared of him until I learned to understand and was able to express myself. My English has never been perfect, or going to be, but at that time it was worse than now and when he found I could speak more with him, he started coming to me and giving me more attention. And from then, I learned more about Sir Alex Ferguson. What he wanted to do, who he was, and the relationship started to be better. He's a man who knows how to manage all characters, all different ages, all different personalities. My personality in that time, I was young, and not easy. I know that and I learned a lot, I changed a lot."

Nani drove Ferguson home after a 2–2 draw at Fulham, having come off the bench and missed a penalty, one which he took instead of Ryan Giggs. "He was my neighbour and when we used to go to London by train his wife or his family used to leave him at the train station so on the way back he had no driver to take him. He was looking for someone who lives close to him to give him a ride. I said, 'OK boss, I'll take you home.' One day I took him home was after a game against Fulham. I drove him back home and he didn't talk to me in the car! In the dressing room he killed me! He said, 'Nani, who do you think you are? Who gave you permission to take the penalty?'" Nani said. Then he killed Ryan Giggs… "'Ryan, why did you let him take the penalty?' Ryan said, 'He grabbed the ball and I let him.' Oh my God, that day was incredible. I took him home and I felt very uncomfortable driving. We got back hours later so I said, 'Boss, I can take you home'? I drove him back home and he still didn't talk to me in the car! I was playing unbelievable with a lot of confidence. We won a penalty, and it was Ryan Giggs who took the penalties. I felt confident. Giggs didn't say anything so I took the penalty and missed!"

Ronaldo, just 20, was informed his father was very ill. Speaking to the Jonathan Ross Show in 2015, Ronaldo said, "In terms of personal stuff I just have to say Thank you for what you did for me. Especially, I remember, the thing that is in my memory, the time my father was sick in hospital very bad, in a coma, and we were in a tough moment in the season. We had important games in the Champions League and league, and I said 'Coach, I need to go and see my daddy, I don't feel good, I want to see my dad.' I was a key player, a very important player. He said, 'Listen your family is the most important thing you have in your life. If you want to go three days, four days, five days, you can go.' When he told me that I feel like, 'Phew, this guy is unbelievable… This is why I love him.' This moment is what I keep with me, because it was the most important moment of my life. He shared it with me, and this is why I respect him. And for me he is the best coach I ever had." Cristiano realised, "It was a family with him in Manchester United. He made me feel like, 'Cristiano, this is your house.'"

Sir Alex's key to success – nothing and no one is above the team. Three most important qualities required for leadership: Control, managing change, observation. Sir Alex explained, "Spotting everything around you, analysing what is important. Seeing dangers and opportunities that others can't see. That comes from experience and knowledge." The most important attribute to a winning mentality? "There's two for me. A will to win. And attention to detail." Steve Bruce wanted to emulate some of Fergie's methods and explains, "He is very, very clever. His attention to detail is fantastic. He's learned from other countries. Brian Kidd was all over Europe five or six years ago, watching different coaching methods and introducing detailed diets. But the one thing I hope I've learned most from Fergie is his unbelievable desire to win, and I think the way you get that across to players is in the way you handle situations, the way people look at you."

Ole Gunnar Solskjaer can't see any manager matching him, "The run of titles that we won under Sir Alex, I don't think that's going to be easy for anyone to emulate or copy," he said. "He was a master of staying at the top. Our challenge is to make sure it is not twenty-six years or more before we win it. We will do everything we can to shorten the distance or go past them."

Fergie is glad he'd retired when he did. "Thank goodness. When I see Liverpool's performances in the last few years, it's been incredible. I've the greatest respect for them." Sir Alex is thrilled that United are once again challenging, "Liverpool verses Manchester United is always going to be the game of the season. Quite simply, they're the two most successful teams in Britain when you add up all the trophies they have had together. It's obvious you have to beat Liverpool to win anything, just as when I was at Aberdeen we had to beat Rangers and Celtic to win anything. That was my mental attitude, and it was exactly the same when I arrived at Manchester United."

Sir Alex turned down Inter Milan and England twice, but that didn't stop the FA trying. Ferguson spoke to Dan Walker, to tell him how the then FA chief executive Adam Crozier made an appointment with Martin Edwards to talk to him about signing his manager. Sir Alex said, "I was in the building anyway and Martin says, 'Just talk to him.' I said, 'No way, I'm not gonna manage England.' And Martin says, 'Just do him the courtesy of speaking to him.' The thing was, why would I leave Manchester United? I was as happy as a landlord at this great club. The motivation was there, you look at the training ground and see all these great players. The motivations were the players, the dressing room, the opportunity to win football matches and the biggest motivation of all was to win football matches and I was definitely at the right club. To sit in the stadium at Old Trafford on a Saturday afternoon with no one in it, or a Sunday morning with no one in it, unbelievable motivation. So there was no way I would have left Manchester United, and the club knew that. There was absolutely no way I would have managed Scotland; other than the fact I couldn't have gone back to Scotland."

Fergie didn't bend to suit anyone, "I have seen success change people overnight and it is not nice. Big-time Charlies, arrogance. They have no time for their roots. I see that in a lot of people. That, to me, is the unacceptable face of football. I have a ruthless streak, and I don't like myself for it. It's always there and has been since I started management at Aberdeen. I'll do anything for my players. If they were to wake me at 5 a.m. in the morning and ask for a lift somewhere, I'd pick them up. But then, don't ask me to be loyal when I have to pick my team. The loyalty I have then is to the club." He also said, "Winning means keeping your job, and it can be a delicate situation. But I tell myself I'm not going to fail in this game. It means making unpopular decisions, but I don't want the chairman coming up to me and saying it's time to call it a day."

Ryan Giggs played under Sir Alex for twenty-three years, he observed, "He was the master of psychology, he was a master at getting the best out of certain individuals, knowing whether to put an arm around, or whether to give them a rocket at half-time or at the end of the game or leave them out knowing that the player would react in a positive way." Giggs felt the full wrath of Ferguson on several occasions. "I fell out with him plenty of times. I mean the amount of times I would say over my career, six or seven times where it was a couple of weeks wages I was fined for talking back, for having an argument. At the time it's not very nice, you're in the dressing room, you've just got beaten or you've had a bad performance. And I just couldn't help myself having a go back. There was definitely fear, especially early on. He mellowed a little bit as he got older, but not a lot. Definitely early on, especially as a young player, he had this cough that you could hear. And if you heard that at our first training ground at The Cliff, you would very often turn the other way. You just didn't want to cross him at eighteen, nineteen, twenty because you never knew what sort of mood he was in. So there was definitely that fear, but ultimately there was always that respect, whether he had a go at you, or you just fell out with him."

Cantona, Keane, Robbo and Ronaldo avoided the 'hairdryer.' "There were three or four players that he never had a go at," Giggs told beIN Sports. "Eric Cantona was one – Bryan Robson, Roy Keane and Cristiano Ronaldo. They did the stuff on the pitch, so he never felt he had to. Eric, there were some games where Eric didn't do anything. He didn't score, he wasn't running around like a Carlos

Tevez or a Wayne Rooney, he didn't have any impact. But he knew sooner or later he would come good. We would be sat in the dressing room thinking, 'He's got to have a go at him, he's got to have a pop at him because he didn't do anything today.' But the next week he'd score the winner, or he would produce a moment of magic, so he handled the big names really well as long as they were doing it on the pitch, he handled them in a different way. He was the master of psychology."

Very early in Giggs' playing career Sir Alex threatened to throw Ryan out of the office after a prank by Bryan Robson, who persuaded Giggs to ask for a club car, "I got stitched up. The first thing that comes to mind is the gaffer's red head, looking at me and wanting to throw me out of the window. Basically I'd played about twenty, twenty-five games. Robbo had never taken the mickey out of me or done any practical jokes, so I trusted him, and I said, 'Robbo, everyone's got a club car.' I think it was Volkswagen Passats at the time and Audis. I said, 'I've played twenty-five games now' and he said, 'Yeah I think you should go and ask the manager. Tell him you've played twenty-five games and to give you a car.' So I've gone knocking on the door and I've said to the manager, 'Listen, boss. I've played twenty-five games now, I think I'm fairly established. What about a club car?' Halfway through the sentence I could see his face changing, and as soon as I said club car, I could see his face was red and he just started swearing at me. He said, 'Club car? You won't even get a club bike. Get out of this office now, before I throw you out!' As I opened the door, half the first team are outside the door. They'd been listening in, looking for a reaction. You live and learn."

Fergie was famed for his motivational speeches. Michael Owen moved to Old Trafford in 2009, winning the only Premier League title of his career. Handed the iconic no. 7

jersey he witnessed Ferguson's methods. Owen recalls a team talk in April 2011, ahead of a Champions League quarter-final against Chelsea. "He never did this, but he got us all into a meeting in the hotel room on the morning of the game. We thought, 'Is he going to tell us the team, are we going to talk tactics?' He basically just went round and spoke to everybody and told the team how special he felt they were, both individually and as a team. He started telling a story about himself and when he was younger and how he grew to where he is now. Then he started talking about how in the future when we get to fifty and sixty and seventy and we see each other again, the bond that we will have because... to go into battle at the highest level against the best players with the highest pressure and to come out on top, that almost forms a bond that will never be broken. When you're in the future and you see somebody, you can actually look them in the eye and think, 'he would have spilled blood for me on that night.' He just went through the scenario. It was just the most emotional and unbelievable team talk that made us all feel a real team before we went to play that game. It was probably the best team talk I've ever been involved in."

Patrice Evra details the speech that fired up his players to make history in rainy Moscow in the final against Chelsea. "[He] gave the greatest speech ever. He didn't talk football. He said, 'Imagine Patrice with his twenty-four brothers and sisters. His parents have to feed them all on a bad street.' He talked about Rooney growing up in a tough part of Liverpool. Carlos Tevez coming from Argentina. He talked about difficulties for other players. He then said, 'This is my victory. We have already won the Champions League. Enjoy the game.' Even now I'm having goosebumps."

Sir Alex's recovery from a life-threatening brain haemorrhage is described in graphic detail in the film,

Sir Alex Ferguson: Never Give In. Sir Alex spent several days in intensive care after falling ill at home in Wilmslow, Cheshire. He was taken to Macclesfield District Hospital and later transferred with a police escort to Salford Royal. Sir Alex feared losing his memory, "Losing my memory was my biggest fear. In the making of this film, I was able to revisit the most important moments of my life, good and bad. Having my son Jason direct this film has ensured an honest and intimate account."

Sir Alex raised £400,000 for the NHS as a thank you. He also wanted to thank well–wishers "for the support you have given me" as he said, "It has made me feel so humble, as have all the messages I have received from all over the world. I want to thank the medical staff at Macclesfield, Salford Royal and Alexandra hospitals. Believe me, without those people who gave me such great care I would not be sitting here today. Thank you from me and my family. The good wishes do resonate very strongly with me."

The film began as a tribute but producer John Battsek, speaking to Screen Daily, commented, "A layer of the film is Sir Alex in recovery, grappling with the threat of the loss of his memory, that being the memory of the greatest football manager that ever lived." The film starts with the audio of the 999 call Jason made early on Saturday 5 May. Neurosurgeon Joshi George, who helped with the treatment, said there was "an eighty per cent chance" he would not survive. "There were five brain haemorrhages that day," Ferguson says. "Three died. Two survived. You know you are lucky. It was a beautiful day, I remember that. I wondered how many sunny days I would ever see again. I found that difficult."

He suffered a setback, when his 'voice stopped.' He said, "I was trying to force it out, but I couldn't get it out. One of the doctors came in and I was crying because I felt helpless."

After working with a speech therapist his voice returned after ten days. "I would have hated to lose my memory. It would have been a terrible burden on my family, if I was sitting in the house not knowing who I am. Two doctors came in and said, 'Write your family's names, your friends' names, your football teams' names, your players' names'. I just kept writing, writing and writing." He revisited some of the notes for the film; it was "impossible to read." When he got home, "all the things were bottled up inside me." Sir Alex added, "It was all opening up and spilling it all out. What you realise is, 'what happens when you die?' I don't remember anything. When I collapsed that Saturday morning, I have no idea what went on. People say I was sat up talking in Macclesfield Hospital before I went to Salford, but I don't remember a thing. I am not sure, when the moment comes and you do die, whether it is the best way to go. The moments when you are on your own, there is that fear and loneliness that creeps into your mind. You don't want to die. That is where I was at. These things did flash through my mind quite a lot."

Fergie was close to perfection with the 1998–99 team. "Perfection? The only thing that's perfect with me is my perseverance. It is just like a game of golf. You play one great game and then the next you are left disappointed. The job here is to try to maintain standards. If the players can create their own and they have a pride in that, a self-motivation, a self-preparation, then the job is much easier. You have to accept that's the way it is. Maintaining standards and a level of commitment."

Sir Alex never got bored with winning, "Well, the alternative is enjoying getting beat! That was not part of my life. Listen, I could encapsulate it in this way. If I'm going to walk into the training ground at Carrington as the manager of Manchester United, and I look out on that football field and I see this fantastic training ground, why wouldn't I want to go in there every day? The only way you can do that is being successful. So, being bored? I was never bored in my life, about anything."

Any regrets? "There's no point in regretting anything. You can maybe make a mistake here, a mistake there. But you can't look upon them as something to regret. You might want to do one or two things again if you had the chance. Maybe changed your mind about something. But nothing serious. Not serious enough to regret. I'm not envious of anyone starting the job, except perhaps of the money they will be earning. But really, the time has flown. You wonder where the years have gone sometimes. Winning the League for the first time. That really opened the door for us. We had waited twenty-six years for it to happen. Since then the club has got stronger. I've enjoyed it, yes."

Brian Kidd, Kiddo and Gaffer, won nine major trophies in six years together. Brian says, "It was good, working with The Boss. He has a laugh and, to be fair, he will say his piece. But he doesn't bear any malice. Did we fall out? Loads of times. But let's just say we had discussions. When I was youth development officer it was the same. I would have views about certain young players and I would stick to my guns. I wouldn't be overawed or worried about The Boss saying what he thought about the player. I would turn back and say, 'What do you know? You don't see him enough.' He used to laugh at that. But fair dos to The Boss. If it came to the crunch he would back me. Our discussions became very few and far between. In my time with The Boss he's certainly mellowed over the years. Whether that's because we had a little bit of success, who knows? But whatever the chemistry was, I have certainly enjoyed working with him. You will have to ask him if he enjoyed working with me. Our backgrounds are similar. I was born in Manchester. Alex was raised in Glasgow. We are both stubborn in certain ways, but we have the same philosophy. You do an honest day's work for an honest day's pay. The Boss was brought up by his parents to believe that and so was I. You don't try to short-change anybody. We both enjoy our jobs and we don't take them for granted. I loved the working relationship we had."

The relationship became soured. Comments in Sir Alex's autobiography suggested Kidd was insecure, a moaner who questioned the signing of Dwight Yorke, proposing John Hartson instead. Kidd's immediate response was that Walt Disney was "trying to buy the film rights to the book as a sequel to *Fantasia*." In time Kidd gave Fergie "the benefit of the doubt". He added, "I will always appreciate what he's done for me."

Kidd paid an emotional tribute to Fergie when his old boss was in intensive care, when, as a member of Guardiola's backroom team at City, he said he was 'indebted' to him for the opportunity he gave him and said everyone at City prayed he pulled through. "He's such an iconic person, as everybody knows," said Kidd. "You think Sir Alex is really indestructible, we've all been brought up with him. What he did for Manchester United was unreal and with the pressure he was under every day to produce. It's phenomenal. Obviously for all of us at Manchester City, he's in our prayers and thoughts – Cathy and the kids – we wish him a speedy and happy recovery and we hope it's a quick one. You know him, you lads have had your run-ins with him, but you knew where he was coming from, he wears his heart on his sleeve. The opportunity he gave me, I'm always indebted to him, God bless him."

Guardiola, who had dinner with Ferguson in Manchester a fortnight before, paid his tribute after some City fans held aloft a banner: 'Football Aside, Get Well Fergie.' "I think Brian can speak better, because Brian knows him very well, but I think Sir Alex, from the very beginning, was always there," said Guardiola. "Him and his wife Cathy, all the family, we hope they'll get well and that he'll recover well as quickly as possible and come back for the United family. All the Manchester City fans in the stadium, you cannot find one person who does not wish the best for an amazing person and an outstanding manager. I was glad to have dinner with him two weeks ago, and hopefully he can recover as quickly as possible."

A Tough Upbringing

Alex Ferguson arrived kicking and screaming into the world, born on 31st December 1941 as World War II air raid sirens wailed and bombers roared in the night sky over Govan, the hardest area in the steely city of Glasgow.

Sir Alex's tough upbringing gave him backbone, resolve, ambition, and obsessive will to win. He says, "You can't forget your upbringing because that's what made me. I remember reading in a newspaper that said, 'Alex Ferguson has done well despite coming from Govan.' It's because I came from Govan that I did well. It's because of the family I had, made sure that food was on the table, that you were representing your mother and your father all the time.

"Football is one of these great attractions for any kid. You see a ball rolling and a kid will run after it and I grew up in the same vein and being given the opportunity to play football and also for myself to be a professional, that started from a humble background. When you are that age you don't think you are going to do it but given the opportunity you seize it."

His roots dictated his relentless work ethic, and a taste for leadership; as a teenage apprentice toolmaker he organised an illegal strike because he thought management was about to cut wages. In a chat with Alastair Campbell, Fergie talked about the impact that came from his upbringing, "My dad was on the left, and so were most people where I came from. I grew up in a very working-class area of Glasgow and I was always very conscious of the sense of community, people and families supporting each other. I grew up believing Labour was the party of the working man, and I still believe that. Then, when I was working in the shipyards on Clydeside, I realised how important it was that people had proper representation and I got involved as a shop steward in the union. I led an unofficial walkout over pay. There was another thing that politicised me even more as an adult, and that was when my mother was dying in November 1986, just a couple of weeks after I took over at United. She was at the Southern General in Glasgow, and it was absolutely dreadful, cladding hanging off the pipes, doctors and nurses overworked, and so little dignity attached to it. All my life I've seen Labour as the party working to get better health care for ordinary people, and the Tories really only caring about the people at the top. The NHS is definitely better after twelve years of Labour."

Asked if it is possible to have wealth and still hold those political views, he said, "Of course it is. I still keep in touch with friends from those days, and I always will. It's true I've earned a lot of money. But I've worked hard, pay my taxes and put a lot back in different ways." In his office at The Cliff training ground, on the cabinet, next to the bookshelves full of yearbooks and United programmes, there were a couple of framed photographs: Fergie with Jack Charlton, with Bob Paisley. A sign pinned on the wall, a tribute to his Glasgow roots, printed in capitals: 'HACUMFIGOVAN.'

In the Amazon Prime film, *Sir Alex Ferguson: Never Give In* released in May 2021 Ferguson spoke about his upbringing, "I used to lie in bed thinking about themes where I could address the players that would make an impact on them. I would talk about miners, shipyard workers, welders, toolmakers, people who've come from poor backgrounds. And I used to ask them, 'What did your grandfather do? What did your father do?' But I have to get the feeling inside them that what their grandfathers worked for and their grandmothers is part of them. And they have to display that meaning. Taking away all the trophies I've won and the great players I've had, I think it's a thing about life. It's a fact of life that where we come from is important. You come out with an identity. I come from Govan, I'm a Govan boy."

Speaking after seeing the final edit of the film, Fergie added, "It was a powerful moment seeing the final cut of the film. There were times which nearly brought me to tears, it was incredibly emotional."

Sir Alex had an insatiable appetite for winning. He explained, "I think it was just a natural thing for me. My upbringing was a lot to do with that, but the important thing was this inner determination that when I entered the field of play, it was to win. Nothing else mattered."

Stein, Busby, Shankly, Sir Alex, all working class Scots, as Fergie observed, "I think we're back to the values we grew up with in the kind of places we came from. Hard work. Teamwork. Strong beliefs. Jock was an incredible guy. I was manager at Aberdeen when he asked me to be his assistant with Scotland as well, so I had eighteen months to see him close up. The two things I remember above all were his humility and his intelligence. He knew everything that was happening in Scottish football, everything. He knew about players I was looking at before I knew it myself."

Fergie rated Stein the greatest and was alongside him the night of the Wales–Scotland match on 10 September

1985 when he had his heart attack and died. "Oh my God. You know, I said a few minutes earlier to the team doctor, 'I'm a bit worried about the Big Man, he doesn't look right' – and then the ref blows his whistle for something and Jock thought it was for the end of the game and he stands up, and that's when it happened and I grabbed him. He was still alive then, but had a second heart attack later, and he died. He was a great man. I learned a lot from him."

Asked if he ever doubted he could accomplish all of his achievements, Sir Alex said, "There were periods when I went through a spell of not winning games but I was brought up in a working-class background. Having doubts never surfaced with me. I was always positive about where I was going. The doubts came from other people, not from me."

Aggressive Centre-Forward

Drumchapel Amateurs and the late Douglas Smith, the founder of the Glasgow club, had a profound effect on a young footballer. Fergie, who unveiled a portrait of his former mentor at the Scottish Football Museum, gave full credit to his early lessons in football and life, "Douglas Smith didn't only teach you about football, he also instilled in you a code of life. Discipline, cleanliness, good time-keeping, no swearing, sportsmanship – and how to be competitive as well. I'd already learnt about punctuality from my father, who was a real stickler. My mum said he opened up the yard every morning because he was always the first at work. So between Douglas and my dad I'm never late for anything to this day. Although we were amateurs, we were treated like professionals. The organisation and preparation for matches were meticulous. I can remember going with Eddie McCreadie, Andy Lochhead and the best young player of all in my days, David Thompson – who went to America to become a songwriter – for Sunday lunch at Douglas's huge mansion. We trooped through his orchard to play football on his private bowling green. He didn't care about your background or religion, only if you could play football."

As an amateur with Queen's Park, aged sixteen, Ferguson described his first match as a 'nightmare,' but scored in a 2–1 defeat against Stranraer. Despite eleven goals in thirty-two games, he failed to maintain a regular place. At nineteen, he moved to St. Johnstone and in a match against his boyhood heroes Glasgow Rangers a hat-trick transformed his fortunes.

Dunfermline Athletic signed him on professional terms in 1964, Fergie scoring sixty-six goals in eighty-nine games. Willie Cunningham is celebrated as one of the heroes of Northern Ireland's 1958 World Cup Finals, he was also mentor to Sir Alex, whose notorious 'hairdryer' was modelled on his former Dunfermline boss. Sir Alex was given seventeen touchline bans as United manager alone.

Ferguson fulfilled his dream move to Glasgow Rangers for £65,000, a record between Scottish clubs. During his two years he scored forty-four goals in fifty-seven games. He left Rangers after the 1969 Scottish Cup, when he was blamed for giving away a goal. He signed for Falkirk, where he became a player coach, but in 1974 left when manager John Prentice took charge and dismissed him from his coaching duties. Alex put in a transfer request and joined west coast side Ayr United, where he finished his playing career after a serious knee injury.

Sir Alex specialised in heading. In the light of the modern-day debate concerning the impact of constant heading of the ball contributing to the onset of dementia he reflects, "Those leather balls. When water got into them, it was like heading a cannonball. Really heavy work. I headed the ball a lot but thank God it's not hit me yet. At the end of the day we have to see what we can do to help. Football has a duty to look at the situation. It's the right thing to do. People like myself owe it to the game to see if there's something we can do. Heading is a part of football that has been there for over 100 years and you can't take it out. But I think it would be easy to reduce it in training... We never used to practise it much anyway — unless we were playing Wimbledon!"

Sir Alex put his voice to one of the many campaigns supporting the fight against dementia in football. He told the *Daily Mail*, "It's littered right throughout the football spectrum. Jeff Astle, Martin Peters, Ray Wilson. And United have had a serious blow themselves with Nobby [Stiles] and Bill Foulkes. It's been very sad. Bobby's [Charlton] not been well for quite a while. The gates have been opened by Nobby's passing and Bobby's diagnosis. They are huge figures. It has to create an awareness. I don't know what the Professional Footballers' Association is doing but the League Managers Association is concerned and [chief executive] Richard Bevan has been fantastic."

Sir Kenny Dalglish and Sir Alex appeared for an event in aid of football dementia research during the lockdown of 2020. Fergie recalled a brutal Glasgow winter in 1969 and a Scottish Reserve Football League Old Firm fixture at Celtic Park. Dalglish was an eighteen-year-old Celtic forward, the 'next big thing', but for 'educational reasons,' was at centre half up against experienced Ferguson, a Rangers striker ten years his senior, who had just been given a run out in the reserves. While marking Ferguson, he turned out his tracksuit pocket, as if to say he had him in it. Ferguson recalled telling him, "You'll need a doctor for this" and promptly scored. Dalglish thought Celtic won 2–0, but he told Fergie, "We actually won 4–1... The St. John Ambulance came on to resuscitate you."

Ferguson mentioned to the Rangers manager that Dalglish might be worth signing. He'd been tipped off by a Rangers player, Alan Miller, who knew him. "And lo and behold he goes and signs for Celtic," Ferguson said. "That was good news! That was a tragedy."

Dalglish recalled Ferguson giving him and his friends a lift into Glasgow in his Austin Cambridge, during his Celtic years. "My feet didn't touch the ground. I was that wee." Rather different words were exchanged when Dalglish pulled out of Scotland's World Cup squad in 1986. Ferguson, still Aberdeen manager while looking after the national side, pinned his faith on Dalglish. Then, one night shortly before the finals, Dalglish phoned Ferguson at home and said he was withdrawing. Ferguson was livid. He got in his car and drove around to cool down. Dalglish explained, "Unless I rested the knee and hardly bent it over the next three weeks, the damage could have been more serious. I phoned Alex Ferguson right away. I felt terrible, not for myself but for him. He had done so much for me that season." Ferguson pointed out that others were willing to go to Mexico after a hard season. Angry words were exchanged.

In 1976, having retired from playing a couple of years prior, he took his St. Mirren team on a three-week pre-season tour of the Caribbean because former chairman Harold Currie, had business links in the trading of whisky. In one friendly game against the Guyana national team ahead of a big World Cup qualifier, they were treating it as a serious warm up game. Their centre-half was giving young Robert Torrance a rough time, which so angered Fergie that it prompted him to remonstrate with the referee from the touchline. When Torrance was again fouled by the same player, Fergie 'went'. "That's it, I'm coming on," Ferguson said to his assistant David Provan. "That big bastard is taking liberties." Provan and Ferguson were kitted out as substitutes for a laugh, but Fergie wanted a bit of the action. When the next cross came in, Ferguson exacted, 'a bit of revenge' on the defender, leaving him 'squealing.' Ferguson went in hard again and was shown the red card. After the game, Fergie told his players to keep tight-lipped about what had happened.

Former United captain and one of the club's greatest legends Martin Buchan tells me, "The first time I encountered Alex Ferguson was on the 8th of October 1966 when, at the age of seventeen years and seven months, I made my debut for Aberdeen Football Club away at East End Park against Dunfermline Athletic. Although he was not my direct opponent (I was man-marking the opposition's play-maker, usually in those days a clever inside-forward of no more than five feet seven inches tall), he made an impression on me with his awkward, all-action, aggressive, all knees and elbows style of play, demonstrating the combative spirit which was to serve him so well in his managerial career. Fast forward to a year and a half later when he was playing for Glasgow Rangers, to an incident for which he has never forgiven anyone who played in an Aberdeen shirt that day. It was their last game of the season, a season in which they were unbeaten, and they just needed to win at home at Ibrox to clinch the Scottish League title. Rangers scored first, then we equalised, then Fergie scored and, incredibly, we scored two more to deny him a League winner's medal as Celtic won their outstanding fixture the following Tuesday. They say Fergie never forgets anything and he certainly hasn't forgotten that day, I've lost count of the number of times he's brought it up out of the blue over the years.

"I moved to Manchester United in February 1972, Fergie retired as a player in '74 and took over as manager of Aberdeen FC in 1978. In 1983 I was granted a Testimonial Match for my eleven years' service at Old Trafford, and I had always wanted the game to be against my former club. It was a bonus that Aberdeen had just beaten Real Madrid in the final of the European Cup Winners' Cup three months previously. Although Alex must have been on United's radar by then, I like to think that my invitation for him to bring his Aberdeen team to Manchester for my game gave the Board a chance to see up close the man who was to go on and become the club's most successful manager.

"Two years later, after a short but enjoyable spell at Oldham Athletic under Joe Royle, I was manager at Burnley FC and was just about to leave home to drive to Turf Moor for the first League game of the season when the phone rang. It was Alex Ferguson. 'Just ringing to wish you all the best for the season and to give you some advice. Never seek confrontations, they will find you.'

"'What do you mean, Alex?'

"'Don't go looking for opportunities to stamp your authority and show who's boss, plenty of situations will arise where you will have to do just that without manufacturing them.'

"'You're three weeks too late, Alex, I twatted ***** **** three weeks ago.'"

Buchan quit after only four months, "I resigned later as I felt that not too many of the players shared the love for and dedication to the game as I had had as a youngster at Aberdeen. I then worked for Puma on the sales force before being appointed football promotions manager and earned many brownie points when Fergie, four or five years into his tenure at Old Trafford, let me sign up the young sensation Ryan Giggs to wear our boots, 'but only for two years', as he knew that Ryan was destined to be much in demand as he developed his precocious talent.

"In later years I would play in the golf days he hosted at the Belfry and latterly Mere Golf Club as part of the fund raising for the Elizabeth Hardie Ferguson Charitable Trust Fund established in honour of his dear mother. One year at the Belfry, my guest and I showed up for the evening function following the golf resplendent in tuxedos and bow ties only to find Sir Alex, as he was by then, and all the other men in lounge suits. My fault, I obviously didn't read the invitation properly. He called us over and said, 'Would you two gentlemen please bring another round of drinks to my table?'

"I once dared to tell, at a time when he had some very skilful if not overly physical strikers, that he needed to sign 'an Alex Ferguson'. I said, 'When I used to play against you, you never gave me and my back four a minute's peace. You were a bloody nuisance, if we weren't chasing you, you were getting in about us, you never let us settle on the ball, you had us looking over our shoulders all the time, we always knew you were around and came off the pitch knowing we'd been in a game.' I think he was quite pleased about that. He carried that ultra-competitive spirit into his management career. His teams played with the same spirit he did, never gave up and gave rise to that wonderful expression 'Fergie Time'.

"I once remarked to him that I marvelled at the way he had the apparent patience to deal with some of the dodgy agents and their sometimes temperamental clients who seemed to be more interested in money and their profiles than in the game. He admitted that he had had to evolve and adapt his approach as a manager to reflect the changing times and the vast increase in players' wages due to the advent of the Premier League and the SKY TV coverage. It has been a privilege to know him over the years as he 'knocked the Scousers off their perch' and put 'the noisy neighbours in their place'. For me, his last League title at Old Trafford was a particular triumph as he won it with a squad which was not quite as accomplished as previous ones."

In 1987, in the middle of his first full season as United manager, his team played Bermuda and a forty-five-year-old Ferguson, along with his assistant Archie Knox, forty, were introduced for the final twenty-five minutes. Knox scored a thirty-five-yarder while Ferguson, the oldest player on the pitch, went close with a header in a 4–2 victory.

Former Scottish manager Craig Brown recalled, "I first encountered Alex Ferguson in a schoolboy trial match, Glasgow v. West of Scotland, when we were on opposite sides. The following year we played together in the Scottish Schoolboys team which played England at Dulwich Hamlet and lost 4–3. I was the captain and I scored with a penalty kick, but I don't seem to remember Fergie scoring – I have a nice photo of that team with the two of us in it. He hasn't changed in all these years. He was always – what shall we say? – fiery, bright, lively and aggressive, but I think the best word to describe him is probably 'engaging'. He's got a compelling personality. You cannot help but like him or hate him. He's got a warmth about him which I think is very much to do with him being a Glaswegian. He's got the Glasgow patter, that's for sure, but he digs in. He was the union representative at most of the clubs he was at and he was quite a militant. I remember him threatening a strike when he was at Falkirk and he wouldn't have thought twice about calling it. He's got a cheeky, opportunist side to him which can be very amusing or very aggravating depending on whether you're with him or against him when it happens. There's no side to him. He's never two-faced. He's right out with what he thinks."

Fergie recalled when he was arrested and jailed after getting involved in a drunken brawl. He was taken to court and fined. He 'always regretted' that period of his life as he had a fall-out with his father. They didn't speak to each other for two years. "I was getting despondent about football because I wasn't a first-team player all the time. My career was going down the pan and I went off the rails a bit. I was going out in town and I started going out on Friday nights even, the day before a game. My dad would say, 'You can't go dancing if you've got a game tomorrow.' That's when we fell out. It got to a point where he said, 'Go your own way and we'll see what happens' – and then we weren't talking to one another. For two years between 1961 and 1963, we didn't talk. One night I went out and I got drunk and I ended up in a fight and in jail. I went to court and got fined £3. I was a bit of a black sheep. That period has always been in the back of my head and I have always regretted it. Here's me with the background and upbringing I had and I surrendered."

Teddy Scott was Aberdeen's kit manager. He observed, "The first time I ever encountered Alex Ferguson was at a reserve game at Pittodrie when he was playing with Falkirk. I had our players together and I was doing my team talk when suddenly the dressing-room door was flung wide open and this fellow breezed in and shouted to Des Herron, who was one of our lads, 'Hi, Des! How're you doing?' And the rest of us just watched amazed while he had a chat with Des and then off he went back to his own dressing room. I asked, 'Who was that?' Des said, 'Oh, that's Alex Ferguson. He's a pal of mine.' Des was a great joker. He never stopped telling funny stories and the word was that he and Fergie and Billy Connolly hung about together and that they gave Billy some of his jokes. Anyway, I certainly didn't think Fergie was going to be my boss one day but when he did come here as manager we seemed to hit it off right away."

It was during his playing career in 1966 that Alex married Cathy Holding, and settled down. They have three sons – Mark, Darren and Jason. Darren, a former Manchester United player, as of 2021 is the manager of Peterborough United.

Early Managerial Career

At the age of thirty-two, Fergie began with a part-time job in June 1974 with East Stirlingshire FC for £40 a week. He moved to St. Mirren to start his full-time management career, where the Saints' team won the Scottish First Division in 1976–77 to begin one of the greatest trophy hauls of all time.

Between 1974 and 1978 he transformed St. Mirren, discovering a number of young players who took the team from the lower half of the Second Division to First Division champions. He spotted young talents like Billy Stark, Tony Fitzpatrick, Lex Richardson, Frank McGarvey, Bobby Reid, and Peter Weir. Looking back at his St. Mirren days, Sir Alex described Jim McLean as a tougher opponent than Mourinho or Wenger. McLean, who passed away at the age of eighty-three, shook up Scottish football along with Ferguson in the 80s.

But Ferguson was sacked by St. Mirren. He sued the club for wrongful dismissal but lost at a damaging industrial tribunal. At Aberdeen he began reeling off league titles, European Cup Winners' Cup and the Super Cup. Sir Alex learned what type of player he needed to make his sides successful. He said, "Some players I had were absolute natural footballers, with natural talent. But there were other players who shared my determination, who maybe weren't the best players, but they made themselves the best players, because they had something inside them too. I go back to one of my first defeats as a manager, at thirty-two years of age. I didn't expect it. I went into the game eyes wide open, that this was going to be easy. We lost 5–2 to Albion Rovers. I was the manager of East Stirling, the players were on £5 a week, or something like that. I came home and I said, 'If I don't get Alex McLeish in my team, I'm not going to succeed.' So I made sure that my players had a mental toughness about them, from that moment on. I believe in instinct. I had a good instinct about players and I had a good instinct about watching players who I maybe wanted to buy. I knew that, looking at certain players, I could see traits that told me they were Manchester United players, or Aberdeen players, or St. Mirren players. I could see that in certain players I watched. Instinct was really important."

Alex McLeish was the bedrock of the Aberdeen granite defence on which Fergie's momentous years at Pittodrie were built. McLeish tells me, "Billy McNeill had given me my debut, but I had only played a couple of games, before he got the call from Celtic, and Fergie arrived. Archie Knox would take the young boys out in the afternoon, to teach them good habits so they would be used to the formation when they got into the first team. It was indicative of how Fergie liked to bring the boys through the ranks. Willie Miller and Willie Garner were the centre halves, but for a big cup tie at Celtic Park, The Boss told me I'd be playing in midfield, 'I want you to be a scarf around Tommy Burns' neck' he told me. He wanted me to mark Tommy. You would describe it in modern terms as a 'holding midfielder' but I must have done it well as he played me there until Willie Garner broke his leg and then I came in at centre half.

"He remembered every single incident in a game, and in one game I was up against the Dundee United centre forward David Dodge and let him go and turn and shoot from twenty-five yards because I was concerned the way Paul Sturrock had made a run. At half time he made some points to one or two players, then he turned to me, 'Alex...' I knew it was coming, here we go, he's remembered that one incident when the centre forward got that shot away... 'Alex, you let the centre-forward come off you the whole f****** half'. Well, I couldn't accept that, and I said, 'He came off me the once, and he would have needed to score a worldie from that distance.' Fergie raised his voice significantly, and clearly he hadn't listened to anything I said, '...the whole f****** half'. I held my hands up and said, 'He won't be doing that again in the second half, boss.'

"It evolved into the 'hairdryer', Sir Alex became a household name, and the whole world got to hear about the hairdryer but back then, it all seemed normal, you didn't expect anything else from the manager. There were many strong characters, like Jim McLean at Dundee United, fiery managers, big personalities and Alex Ferguson was to become one, due to this insatiable lust he had for winning, which rubbed off on every one of his players. He inherited a good team, but he fleshed it out and put the finishing touches to it, but mainly instilled that winning attitude, his man-management was his big strength. His other big strength was the ability to adapt as the game changed, so did he, he adjusted his approach.

"I can still laugh at the day we worked really hard in pre-season training at the Gordonstoun boarding school where Prince Philip was educated in Moray in Scotland, well known for its sports. Fergie said, 'You've worked so hard, tomorrow we are going to have a game of cricket.' That came as a shock, as we were not renowned for our cricket in Scotland. Fergie found out that the sports master lived in the area, so as the school was empty at that time of year we were able to use the dormitories. He told us, 'he's coming to kit you all out in cricket whites.' That sounded pretty flash for us Scots. Alex and Willie Miller opened the batting for their team, and Fergie had been boasting that he was going to be like Geoffrey Boycott and be at the crease for a long time. Halfway through the first over, one of our young lads bowled the gaffer, the stumps and bails went flying all over the place. But Fergie didn't walk. We all stood there awkwardly, but Stuart Kennedy an international full back also had played cricket at a high standard, and knew all the rules, and said, 'errr, boss, why are you not walking as your stumps and bails are all over the place?' Fergie turned to him and said, 'Canne be out in the first over.' Everybody just looked at each other. We let him get on with it and left him in. A couple of overs later he was gone. But his refusal to accept he was out was typical of his need to win."

Doug Ellis passed away at the age of ninety-four in October 2018. Doug enjoyed recounting the tale of Ferguson and the cross-border transfer tribunal over the signing of Neale Cooper from Aberdeen. Villa manager Graham Turner, Ferguson, his Aberdeen chairman and his son were present at the tribunal as Ellis took up the story which he once told me, "The four-man panel of judges all came from Ireland and the usual procedure in these tribunals, which I might add I've chaired several times, is that the buying club makes its representations followed by the other club. Each party makes their points separately and then they both go before the panel to be told the price and the conditions of sale, and there is no form of appeal. Once we had both made our cases, we were in the corridor together outside the tribunal room. I turned to Alex and his chairman and said, 'Look, we're in the hands of these people... we are in football together, so whatever their decision we won't dispute it, argue about it or have any animosity toward each other about it.' They nodded in agreement and we all shook hands on what was a gentlemanly way of going about a difficult situation for everyone. Then we were all called in to hear the verdict. The price was set at £500,000. At just half a million for Neale Cooper we were absolutely delighted. Alex went mad, raving mad, absolutely potty; he went red in the face and started shouting and bawling. The deputy chairman was tapping him on the knee under the table and urging him to calm down and keep quiet and said to him, 'Remember what we had agreed.'

"Alex got up to storm out. I got up to stop him and offer him my hand. He refused to shake it. But I am sure he has matured since then! And before anyone gets the wrong impression, we have been great friends since then, even though there are times when I cannot understand a word he says – and that's saying something, considering I had Tommy Docherty as one of my managers." Doug had the utmost admiration for Ferguson, "Alex is a winner. Certainly Alex's position was in jeopardy at one stage and he turned it all around."

Gordon Strachan knows exactly what drives Sir Alex on, what makes him tick, and what triggers the most outrageous rants in any dressing room having seen it all from close up. "Ferguson was guided by the same principle: you're on his side or the wrong side. There is also a softer, caring side to his character. All the stuff about teacups flying is true. He would rant and rave, then his players would go into the lounge and he'd charm the wives, chatting away as if nothing had happened. But he remembers a slight. He once accused a group of journalists of cheating during a pop quiz on an Aberdeen Euro trip."

Strachan recalls accompanying his manager on road trips to watch other games when he had to endure a tape of 'some horrendous Glasgow singer!' It reached the stage when that tape went 'missing', and Gordon professed to have an idea where it was! Strachan recalls far more important tapes his Aberdeen boss insisted on him listening to. Tapes of Bill Shankly. Gordon tells me, "These were the days before football was wall to wall on TV, so if you wanted to watch a game, we got in the car, and drove. Not very far as I recall, games in Arbroath or Brechin. It was probably three or four times I shared the car with my manager at the time. He saw me as a young player at Aberdeen who wanted to learn more about the game, and he would put on tapes of Bill Shankly and tell me to listen carefully to what he was talking about. Shankly would talk about discipline and never letting your team mates down. Shanks considered it sacrilege to let either your family or your team mates down, and that was Fergie's principles and key message to his players.

"We had a camaraderie at Aberdeen. If there was a reserve game on, no matter how freezing it might be, all the first team turned up and watched that game sitting together, and Fergie, well, he'd be there as well sitting in front of us. It was a wonderful place, and Fergie brought the success he enjoyed at St. Mirren to Aberdeen and took it on to Manchester United. When he used to live in Aberdeen and had to watch players he would be travelling hundreds of miles – he must have lived in his car. For someone who is such an experienced driver, I must say it's a nightmare to be his passenger! He is so anxious to pass every car ahead of him that he gets right up close to the car in front. For Alex time is of the essence."

Strachan recognises the stress of management but spotted that 'anger was his energy.' Gordon explained, "That's what he needed to keep him ticking over. You have to have the stomach to keep going. I call it the anger to keep on. Sir Alex always had that anger. Oh aye, he had it. There is nothing wrong with anger, anger was his power. You must be stubborn. If you are right eighty per cent of the time the other twenty per cent doesn't matter. Ferguson was stubborn. Arsene Wenger too. All the greats. Don't be swayed. And if you don't have it then don't do it.

"You probably don't appreciate the sacrifices that he had to make to be him but now that I look back, I can thank him for it. Yes, thank him. At the time you think, 'This is a bit rough.' Sometimes it was great when it was someone else getting it in the neck, because it wasn't you, although you did feel sorry for the one getting it! The worst I experienced was after a European game in Transylvania. If anybody was in that dressing room at the same time as me, they would describe it the same way as I would – 'iconic'.

"The game was much simpler back in those days, in fact it was much simpler through the 60s, 70s, 80s and even the 90s, We all played the same way, each player was up against his opposite number, so the winger was up against the full back and so on, but in Europe you had to tinker slightly tactically. We were three up from the first leg and I questioned the tactics in the dressing room. Stupid thing to do. I knew I was going to get it something terrible, so I've no idea why I did it."

While that was a personal 'worst' dressing down in a dressing room, it doesn't even compare to the way Fergie laid into his players in a live TV interview after actually winning a Cup Final! Gordon tells me, "We were all in the dressing room listening to it, and couldn't believe it, as our manager was live on TV. It was the '83 Scottish Cup Final, and we had actually just won it, and the week before we had lost the League by a point and beaten Real Madrid. But after winning this final, Fergie said apart from Willie Miller and Alec McLeish, none of the rest deserved our medals. Fergie said we were a disgrace, our performance was horrendous, he said he would get rid of us all. You really do need to treat yourself and find this interview on YouTube. Fergie goes on for about twenty minutes. It was great TV. It was alright for big Alec and Willie, they just had to kick it up the field, in midfield we had to make the play happen, and so I would invariably be on the receiving end of things from the manager. To this day big Alec says to me that I couldn't have that medal, because I wouldn't have dared go up and collect it. Of course I did collect it. Then he says, 'Still got that medal I won for you?'

"Do you know, it was a pleasure to have been involved despite that tirade against us. You can't dislike Fergie. A couple of days after his rant, it doesn't linger. Back training on Monday, and by Tuesday we are preparing for the next game. There was no negativity, it was all about our relationship and that was exceptional as a group of players. In fact, I feel blessed to have been part of it all, even all the madness. I was actually lucky to have been there with the world's best manager, nine years working with him. Yes, he was indeed the best manager ever.

"But all that madness now gives us something to talk about, and in fact, roll about laughing about. All that chaos and fear is now laughter about what it was like, what we did, forty years ago. We now all get on together, enjoy each other's company, and we all laugh together when we recall what went on but looking back on it all, and I have done sitting outside an Italian restaurant with Fergie. It was a lovely sunny day we spent time outside that Italian restaurant talking about old times, with people walking past laughing thinking, 'what are those two doing together, they don't like each other.' It was really hugely hilarious at times. Even Fergie now looks back and thinks some of the things he did it weren't brilliant! At the time it felt this is as bad as it gets, but now you realise there was a bond created, the players came together, and that bond united the players. Maybe Alex now looks back and might feel a touch embarrassed by some of it, but as I told him, he doesn't need to worry about any of it. In fact, you now realise we experienced some great moments and even better, we have something to look back on and talk about. It all makes me feel a wee bit better about all of it. It was daft days, the players were raging, I was raging, but now we just roll around laughing about it. He could certainly be a bit tetchy with reporters, but you have to realise you need to admire managers because of all the stuff they have to put up with at times."

Fergie and Strachan did fall out, but now no animosity exits, they delight in each other's company, Gordon reminiscing, "We ended up laughing about it all, and couldn't remember half of it, so much went on back then, we forgot loads of it, but reminded each other about it, and understanding its significance. I am sure he enjoyed it, and later we texted each other." The bad blood started when he signed a pre-contract agreement with Cologne against his manager's wishes. Eventually Strachan went to United rather than Germany, but Fergie didn't like the way he left United. Later, reunited at Old Trafford, he joined Leeds by the time the glory arrived.

Ferguson said in his autobiography that Strachan, 'Couldn't be trusted an inch.' Strachan now tells me,

"Fergie had a tough time when he first arrived at Old Trafford as he had to redefine so much of what went on there. At first it didn't work out, and he knew he had to take control of the dressing room which meant the end of the biggest influences such as Paul McGrath, Robbo [Bryan Robson] and Norman Whiteside. He then had to mould the kids into the direction he wanted. He had incredible drive and determination to make it all work. It's much easier to be a manager now than back then, when he was in charge of everything from recruitment to the coaching. He moved people on until he was entirely happy that he had his own players there. It can be tricky when, as a manager, you bring with you one of your ex-players, especially into such a competitive environment as Manchester United, and even more so with a dressing room full of new players. Maybe that's why if there was a barrage from the manager, that barrage came my way! When I looked around you could see the other players' expressions as if to say, 'Wooh, that's a bit steep.' They might also be thinking while he's had a go at him, he's not having a go at someone else. Leaving Old Trafford was fine, United went on to win the League, and I went on to win the League with Leeds.

"Yes, of course, we had fall outs from time to time, but that doesn't stop me understanding why they happened, especially when later on in life you become a manager yourself. You come to realise, it's not just about me, it's about everybody, that the manager cares about the team, and that's why he does it. I love this modern term, 'The manager has lost the dressing room,' in our day, he lost five of us every weekend! But by Tuesday we were over whatever else was said on the Monday in training, and we were ready to go for the next game."

Yet, Strachan recalls a recent text during lockdown. "He wanted to know if I was watching this thing on TV about

Aberdeen in the early 80s. I said I'd fast forward past the 1983 Cup final..."

Ferguson's son Darren managed at Peterborough with Strachan's son Gavin as his assistant, and that paved the way to reunite the pair again. Strachan is pleased to be back on first name terms and tells me how much he rates his old manager's achievements. "Everybody loves the comparison game, but we all know how hard it is to make comparisons in football between different eras as the game has changed so much. When Sir Alex started out everybody played the same formation, there might have been a wee change in the formation, but tactics weren't paramount, it was more about man management than the technical side. But Sir Alex didn't just achieve at Manchester United. He was incredible at St. Mirren and Aberdeen. If you ask anyone at St. Mirren what was their best ever time, they will say it was Fergie's time. Same at Aberdeen, and the same at Old Trafford. Cloughie had two journeys, created two of the best team there has ever been at Forest and Derby, but Fergie did it at three clubs, and for me that ranks him as the no. 1."

Billy Stark played under Fergie at St. Mirren and then Aberdeen. He recalls how Fergie used reverse psychology, "The year we won the title in 1985, we had played at Celtic Park and I missed a penalty that day. Davie Provan curled in a free-kick for Celtic to win it 2–1. The following week in training he sort of sidled by me and just said, 'I hope that doesn't cost us the title,' which was a big thing. He just mentioned it in the passing, but it stuck in your mind and you thought 'Wow.' Whether that was extra motivation – because that was my best season in terms of goalscoring and obviously we won the league at the end of it – I'll never know. But he had those wee psychological things. He seemed to be able to find the right words at the right time."

Archie Knox was one of Fergie's closest aides, assistant at Aberdeen and Old Trafford, "I didn't know Alex that well, but he turned up for a reserve game and asked for a word. I took him into the office at Forfar and he just asked, 'How would you like to be my assistant at Aberdeen?' I said, 'That would be great, I'm up for it.' He asked when I could start and I just said, 'Tomorrow.'

"Did I see a difference in him from Aberdeen to United? No. He was so focused with what he wanted to do with young players. He put the scouting infrastructure in at Old Trafford and said to the scouts, 'If any of them sign for someone else I want to know something about it.' So then we started to get Beckham, Butt, Giggs, Scholes and the Neville brothers coming through. Alex would always have one of the young players that we were hoping to sign, or had just signed, up to a game with their parents for lunch and a chat. When we signed Beckham, he would come to all of our games in London with his mum, dad and sister, and would also come to the team hotel the night before a game. The first thing he said to me when we went into Old Trafford was, 'We need to get to know everyone in this place, from the stewards, the women in the office and the kitchen workers.' We used to go in in the morning and the two ladies who worked in the laundry would make us a cup of tea before we headed to training. It was a case of making sure everyone had a part to play, that we were all in it together. It was the same at Aberdeen, he knew everybody."

Lou Macari is well placed to draw comparisons between the legendary Jock Stein, for whom he played for at Celtic, and the way Sir Alex developed. Lou tells me, "Statistics tell you, not that I'm a slave to stats, that Sir Alex is the greatest. You don't actually need to study the stats, his record is pretty black and white. What he achieved at

Manchester United will never be beaten. There will never be another Manchester United manager who will equal what he's done.

"I never played for Sir Alex, but I got an inside track into what makes him tick while playing at Celtic under Jock Stein, as Sir Alex worked under Jock with the Scotland team and was on the bench with him at Cardiff when Jock had his heart attack. Just like Jock, Sir Alex cultivated a lot of the kids when he came to Old Trafford. For me, Sir Alex was Jock Stein Mark II. Jock was the first British manager to win the European Cup and he did it with the basis of his team were home grown, and even came from in and around Glasgow. There were no fancy transfers, no £40m players arriving every five minutes and not even being right for the team. Jock got the right players, who he thought could do something special and Sir Alex had the same pattern. We were known as the Quality Street Gang at Celtic Park. You couldn't piss him around, you had to get your finger out, and that is what Sir Alex demanded at Old Trafford with his Class of '92. On the bench or at the training ground, they would be bawling and shouting at the players, leaving people in no doubt who was in charge. Training sessions were tough with plenty of tackles and aggression. It was Mission Impossible to replace the Lisbon Lions but Jock's view was if you are good enough you are old enough, and Sir Alex had the same principle. At Celtic Park, Jock was in charge, not the directors or owners or officials, they didn't have a say in anything, they wouldn't dare, and that is the model Sir Alex worked to. Sir Alex was Mr Old Trafford. Who would have thought a manager would come along to surpass what Jock Stein did, but one did, Alex Ferguson, and what he did was bigger and better."

Macari would meet up regularly with Ferguson at Old Trafford, "Always a friendly smile and warm handshake.

He would relish reminding you of something that happened in the past that you were involved in. He's an expert, he'd tell you things that happened in games that you had long forgotten. He has an encyclopaedic knowledge of football."

Fergie banned players from daring to speak on the bus heading back to Aberdeen from Liverpool in 1980 after a humiliating European Cup defeat, threatening to issue fines if anyone tried lightening the mood. After winning at Pittodrie, Liverpool welcomed Aberdeen to Anfield where they had not lost for seventy-six matches. Liverpool extended that record with a 4–0 win, and Fergie was fuming after his first visit to Anfield as a manager. Writing in his book, *A Light in the North* he said, "Towards the end of the game I told Willie Garner – I was still banned from the bench and Willie was acting as a runner for me – that we might as well put on young Neale Cooper for the experience. And I said, 'While you're down there, tell the referee to blow the bloody whistle!' That summed up how I felt. I was never so glad to get a game out of the way in my whole life."

Shortly before his death from motor neurone disease in 1987 Chris Anderson, the one-time vice-chairman of Aberdeen, recalled the club's decision in giving Fergie his big break, "First of all we brought in Ally McLeod in 1975 and won the Scottish League Cup more or less right away. His whole attitude was magical. He breathed new life into us and the city and everybody was dancing on air. When he left to take charge of Scotland we decided that we now had a base to build on and that we should have somebody with a track record as a player. That man was Billy McNeill. After little more than a season Celtic asked him to replace Jock Stein. We analysed it clinically and coldly and we could see that Alex Ferguson was a man who fitted our profile. There were some in the game that thought we were daft and crazy to appoint Alex Ferguson. But we didn't need someone with a great record as a player; we needed a manager with an abundant and wide knowledge of the game – a top coach."

Eric Black joined Aberdeen as a sixteen-year-old in 1980, two years after Fergie had been appointed, "My feelings were of awe and apprehension whenever Fergie was about because he had a reputation as a fiery and intimidating personality, but to his credit he was not a fearsome figure, at least as far as he dealt with the young lads. At that age it is easy to feel ignored at a club or that the manager is only interested in the older players, but Fergie's philosophy was that if we felt looked after and believed we were also part of a big club then we would be encouraged to do more. There was a change in attitude when I went full time and a certain fear factor came into play. If he wasn't happy with your performance he would certainly be critical and sometimes scathing. I didn't enjoy it at all but now that I work with young players myself I can relate to his methods. It can be very painful to be criticised in front of other people and we would sometimes get angry at it but, of course, nobody would ever say it to his face. I certainly would not have argued back even if I disagreed with something he might be saying. But you have to say his methods worked. When you knew he would tear you to shreds for a careless performance you did everything you could to make sure you avoided being a target which, of course, meant that he was getting through to us the message about concentrating all the time. His most important traits are a will to win and ruthlessness in dealing with anything or anybody who might get in the way. Mind you, there were times that his temper and anger were an act.

"I sometimes saw him two minutes before he was to go into the dressing room and he would be fine, chatting with people and telling jokes. Then he would turn around, walk into the dressing room and blast somebody to the end of the earth. The trouble was, as a player you couldn't be sure exactly when there was a bit of acting involved or when he was deadly serious, so again it was an example of how he could keep people on their toes. Tactically, he has the gift of seeing problems or advantages in a game very quickly and he knows how to change it right away. In training he kept himself back and he used to leave most of it to Archie Knox. Archie would be hands on and take control so that Fergie was able to stand back, which in coaching is perfect because if you become too involved you don't see the overall picture, the reaction of the players, whether they're really listening to you. He would tell us that such and such a journalist had written this about us in a newspaper and then just before we had a game we would see the cutting pinned up in the dressing room. Or he would have his rants about the bias towards the west of Scotland in the press and say sarcastically that the number-one reporters were up from Glasgow so we had better try to play well that day. He used whatever worked."

Wife Cathy observed after United's first championship win, "I could not believe how coolly he took everything. He really is a changed man since we came south of the border. When he was manager of Aberdeen, Alex was really hard to live with … but not any longer."

Wanted by Spurs and Arsenal

The former Spurs chairman Irving Scholar might have changed the course of history by recruiting Alex Ferguson. Scholar told me how Ferguson had given his word and had shaken hands on a 'done deal' to succeed Keith Burkinshaw.

Scholar was a dedicated and authentic Spurs fan. On taking control of his boyhood club he went in search of the man he believed would secure Spurs' future. "Keith Burkinshaw wanted to leave at the end of the season. He had made that clear. A very important decision had to be made. There was one person at the time who looked to be one of the real up-and-coming stars of the game – Alex Ferguson at Aberdeen. His record in Scotland was nothing short of exceptional. He was the first manager in modern times to break the Old Firm stranglehold, and in addition to that achieved something that very few Scottish managers had ever done, which was to win a European trophy when Aberdeen beat Real Madrid in the final of the Cup Winners' Cup. Even so, he was not really recognised at the time by people south of the border and would not have been someone who would have readily sprung to mind as a manager for a club in

England. Yet it seemed to be an opportunity that one had to try to explore.

"Quietly I sounded him out to see whether he would even give consideration to the possibility of coming to Spurs. I had heard one or two whispers on the grapevine that maybe it would be a possibility. Strangely enough, we played Bayern Munich that season in the UEFA Cup and the president of the German club spoke with clear admiration of Alex Ferguson as a potential future Bayern manager! His reputation had begun to spread into Europe. I was delighted to discover when I did sound him out through some associates of mine that Alex's response was positive."

Scholar and Ferguson selected a suitable venue to meet. Ferguson travelled to Paris from Aberdeen, while Scholar travelled from Monaco. Scholar continued, "A meeting was arranged out of the way in Paris so we wouldn't be recognised or hassled. I spent a day listening to his thoughts and aspirations relating purely to football. He was an interesting character and clearly very hungry to succeed in the future. The meeting went exceptionally well and I felt an immediate affinity with him. He gave me the distinct impression that he was a very clear thinker who knew what he wanted and how he would go about getting it. He had the ability to fill you with confidence. You just knew that wherever he went, he would succeed in the future. Over the ensuing few weeks the discussions quietly continued, finally reaching a point where all outstanding matters, financial and otherwise, had been settled and there were no matters left open apart from the signature on the contract.

"Alex made it clear from the very beginning that he wanted the late Dick Donald, the Aberdeen chairman at the time, whom he saw very much as a father figure, to be taken into consideration. He felt that the whole affair had to be handled very delicately with the club because of his special relationship with the chairman. He didn't want to let him or the club down. I respected that. In fact, I admired it. Nevertheless, matters progressed and there was a further meeting with him in Paris. This time I brought along another Spurs director at that time. It was at this meeting that Alex Ferguson and I finally shook hands on the agreement that he would become our next Spurs manager. Discussions would then commence with Aberdeen and it would be announced early in the summer of '84. During all our discussions we both made it clear that once we'd shaken hands there would be no going back. I was to be alerted by Alex exactly when would be the most appropriate time to make the formal approach to Aberdeen, but it was also agreed that he would lay the ground in advance. Unfortunately, Alex Ferguson finally advised me in May that he couldn't go ahead with it because he felt he would be letting his chairman down."

Scholar is a close friend of the one-time United chairman, Martin Edwards. Scholar was delighted when Ferguson brought so much success to Old Trafford, but he couldn't resist telling Martin about his attempts to sign Ferguson. Scholar recalls, "Alex hadn't been the manager at Old Trafford very long when I told Martin Edwards that Alex had actually shaken hands with me on an agreement to become Spurs' manager. Initially he couldn't believe it and rang me a couple of weeks later. He had asked Alex whether it was true. Bearing in mind Alex is such a stickler about his word being his bond and not letting people down, Martin was convinced that Alex wouldn't agree with my version of events. Martin told me that Alex's reaction when he confronted him with it said it all!"

Scholar applauds Martin for sticking with Ferguson when the fans were calling for his head. "Martin, like myself, had enormous faith in Alex and even when things were not going well he stood firmly behind him, ignoring at times quite vociferous supporters who wanted him sacked. In fact, I clearly remember one game that Spurs played at Old Trafford in a League Cup tie in October 1989. It was the day Terry Fenwick broke his leg. We beat United 3–0, with Gary Lineker getting one of the goals, and the atmosphere among the crowd was so hostile at the end of the match that when Martin Edwards was walking down the directors' box to the exit two or three fans tried to climb a barrier to attack him. I was walking right behind him. He was lucky they were intercepted in time by security men. Strangely enough, that was the last time they lost a cup tie at Old Trafford that season as they went on to lift the FA Cup in May.

"Alex is in a way a manager ahead of his time." Scholar continues, "He is a great admirer of the European style of football. When we met in Paris first of all to discuss his ideas on the game, he was talking clearly of the mixture of Continental skills and how they can be combined with the best part of the English game, and how if they could be integrated you would have a highly successful team in a very modern style. That is what Alex set out to accomplish and he achieved just that.

"I remember ringing Martin Edwards after Manchester United finally broke their twenty-six-year duck and won the championship, and I said to him, "Now you've managed to achieve it once, I'm absolutely certain you will go on and repeat it two or three times." A lot of credit should go to the board of Manchester United for that, and to Martin in particular because it's normal in this game for supporters to get the manager sacked, but they stood firm and had belief in Alex's ability and their own judgement and they have been proved one hundred per cent correct."

Scholar has met Ferguson since. "Yes, I have bumped into him quite a few times, and I would say that we have remained friends. In fact, I rang him for advice when we were going to buy Richard Gough. I said to him, 'You know the Scottish scene better than anybody...' I felt I could trust his judgement and trust that he would give me a valid assessment. He told me all about Richard Gough. He told me, 'Richard is a big winner in Scotland and if you could get him, don't hesitate.' I took his word and a few days later Richard Gough signed for Spurs."

Scholar's successor as Spurs chairman, Lord Sugar told me, "Alex Ferguson has my utmost admiration for what he has achieved at Manchester United. Frankly I can't say I know him well. I've met him on two or three occasions and spoken to him for no more than a combined hour. Even so, it was long enough for Alex to make a firm impression on me. He had a very, very shrewd look about him; he looked as though he was in total control, and of course he is. He deserves your respect for his achievements alone. But he struck me as a personality and a character most unlike the popular view of him. I enjoyed our little chats and found him a man with a good sense of humour who enjoyed a laugh and a joke. It may be that so many people find him abrasive because they continually harass him with questions about the obvious. You know how it goes, 'Are you going to win the title?' or 'Will Manchester United win the cup?' It's the sort of thing, if you're asked often enough, that's bound to be infuriating. Perhaps we enjoyed a reasonable rapport because I asked him about things unconnected to winning the championship or the FA Cup.

"Jokingly, I asked him how he has managed to pinch so many talented youngsters from under our noses –

don't forget that David Beckham was first associated with our club. He retorted by wanting to know how we got one or two that he'd wanted! It was all good banter and he was able to laugh about it. There were certainly no hostilities whenever we met." Sugar was impressed by his commitment, "He is a very hard-working person and has built a successful team without breaking the Bank of England to do it. Far too often fans think the only solution is to throw money at it, but Alex Ferguson has proved that a club needs a foundation based on a youth structure and we are trying to do that at Spurs with our own academy of football.

"He commands respect from his players. You never hear of a Manchester United player mouthing off in the media about their manager and his methods, and he also comes across as a shrewd and knowledgeable football man whenever he is interviewed on television. But most important is his record. We can all talk day and night about our ideas and ways of doing things. It is incredible what Alex Ferguson has achieved. The bottom line is the record speaks for itself."

It was not just in the corridors of power at Tottenham that Sir Alex found admirers in north London. Former Arsenal vice-chairman David Dein explains, "I am a great admirer of Alex and what he has achieved at Manchester United. The club went through a long barren patch before his arrival, and though it took a few years before he won his first trophy he then delivered the title for the first time in around a quarter of a century."

Dein considered recruiting Ferguson before Arsenal appointed one of their old boys, George Graham. Dein opens up the secrets of the Highbury boardroom to reveal how he considered Ferguson as one of the Gunners' managerial candidates to take over from Don Howe. He tells me, "Yes, we nearly employed Alex. I met him a couple of times in Aberdeen before he went to Manchester United. I had a number of meetings with him and he was seriously considered for our position, but in the end we decided to go for an ex-Arsenal man in George Graham. We took George from Millwall even though he was relatively untried. We didn't offer the managerial post to Alex Ferguson. I have met Alex more than a dozen times over the years and I have always found him to be an extremely astute man."

Old Trafford: The Signed
and the Unsigned

Sir Alex went out on a high with his 13th Premier League trophy, a record that will probably never be equalled. He amassed thirty-eight trophies at United and fifty in all including those won at St. Mirren and Aberdeen. He described his epic Old Trafford reign as an "Honour and a privilege." He became a director and ambassador after he formally retired after United's match with West Bromwich Albion on May 18 – his 1,500th in charge.

When Ferguson first took the reins, he needed to stamp out the drinking culture. He did so and those who were the outcasts, the victims still hold him high regard, as Norman Whiteside told me, "Sir Alex Ferguson and I had and still have a very good relationship. We both respected each other and were honest with each other. That's what made our relationship work. He is a very well-read man, someone who you would have at a dinner party."

Fergie explained, "The first thing I had to do at Manchester United was rebuild the club. I think the club is the essence of the venture of making a successful team. Most managers go to a football club because it's a 'result' industry. They're there to turn around the fortunes of the first team, that's why they get the job. I never thought that way. My philosophy was to build a football club." It was a haul to get an archetypal sleeping giant back to the top, but even harder staying there, as he explained, "When you're at the top... and you've got there and the view is beautiful. In normal circumstances you have to come down the mountain. Not in football. At Manchester United you have to stay up there and look at the view – you can't come down."

Sir Alex even helped give players massages during his early days according to Clayton Blackmore, who spent eight years with Fergie. He recalled how Fergie and his assistant Archie Knox mucked in when needed, "The manager was way ahead of his time. He started bringing us in on a Sunday to get rid of the lactic acid, which was never done before. With the amount of staff we had, he was massaging our legs. The gaffer, Archie and Jim McGregor. I mean, he's washed my legs once before. As soon as he touched them, it was in the newspapers the next day. We didn't have staff, did we? We only had Jim McGregor, the physio, then we had Sir Alex and Archie. On a normal day, if he wasn't doing it, the kitman would. Normally he had way too much stuff to do."

Fergie was so strict that he didn't speak to him for a month after he missed the start of pre-season to go on his honeymoon. "It was a tricky one because I'd just got married and I had organised to go away. He brought us back a week earlier than what Ron [Atkinson] used to do, so I told the gaffer and he said it was fine. I came back and he didn't speak to me for a month. First time he came up to me, he said, 'You're playing against Spurs tomorrow,' and that was that."

Paul Parker recalls, "Steve Bruce's wife Janet was in hospital having a back operation and we were playing. Brucey left his mobile phone on during the game. We came in at half-time and things weren't going well at Old Trafford. So we are sitting in the dressing room and Steve's phone goes off. We are all sitting there wondering whose it was. I knew it wasn't me, and I knew it wasn't Denis [Irwin] as his phone was never switched on. Big Pete [Schmeichel] straight away as normal was like, 'It wasn't me' and maybe his eyes are giving away who it was. Everything went quiet and you just looked at Brucey and his face and persona said, 'It was me.' The gaffer ran across, grabbed the phone and had a go at Steve Bruce. He had a go back trying to tell him his wife was in hospital. The gaffer said, 'I don't care if your wife is in hospital' and threw the phone against the wall towards the bin. Smashed the phone!"

Terry Gibson was brought to the club by Big Ron Atkinson and was one of the squad that Fergie inherited, a large number that the new manager had earmarked to move. Terry was sold to Wimbledon but he tells me it was in the most bizarre of circumstances as he headed off back to London to form part of the infamous Crazy Gang alongside Vinnie Jones, Dennis Wise, John Fashanu and Lawrie Sanchez that shocked Liverpool in the 1988 FA Cup final.

United were second from bottom in the old First Division after a disastrous start saw Big Ron sacked, and Terry thought he was about to embark on a new start as he wasn't played that much by Atkinson, feeling that Big Ron had his favourites. To his surprise, he didn't get more of a chance with the new boss, even though the regime and attitudes changed dramatically. Terry tells me, "I had a blazing row with the manager. I was brought by Ron Atkinson, yet he didn't give me much of a chance and I thought with the arrival of Fergie I would get more opportunities, but my confidence had gone, I'd been there a long time, and it wasn't working out for me. It was a year after my arrival that I made my home debut against Arsenal, and that was only my fourth game.

"So when the new manager arrives you think it might be different, but then you read in the papers all the lists they publish about the players likely to go with the arrival of the new man. Of course, it is all speculation, but at that time, it was a pretty long list, and my name was on it. Because my confidence was shattered, I believed it, and actually sold my house even though I hadn't actually asked for a transfer or was officially told that I would be sold. I was in a reserve team to play against Chesterfield's first team, but because a United X1 were playing there, the place was packed out with 10,000 fans. The journey there was horrendous, we arrived ten minutes before the kick-off and we were three-down before half time. We actually won 4–3 but myself and John Sivebaek were the only senior players amongst all the kids.

"The next day, back at training, I thought we would all get a pat on the back for the fabulous comeback and winning 4–3. Instead, the manager gave all the kids a real dressing down. I stood up for them. I said, 'Be fair, we got to the ground so late, and having a go at them is a bit harsh.' Well, Fergie went berserk. I went berserk back and people all over The Cliff heard it for some distance. I told Fergie, 'You can shove football up your arse, I've had enough of it.'"

Having sold up in the north assuming he would be sold, Gibson's wife was back in London. Terry went on, "I went back to the hotel room, where I was all on my own, the wife and my daughter back in the south, it wasn't a good point in my life. But I thought it all over and went back into training the next day with the intention of apologising to the manager for my behaviour. No mobiles back then, so I got a call from my wife at the hotel, just before I left.

She told me that Bobby Gould was on the phone and wanted to speak to me. So I called Bobby and he told me that having just taken over at Wimbledon as manager, he wanted to sign me, and I told him I would be keen to join him. Even though it would be less money I really wanted to kick start my career again and get some regular football.

"As I made my way to training, and to the manager's office, I thought I had blown my chance of a move with my outburst. I saw the manager, and I apologised. He said, 'I understand where you are coming from, you spoke your mind, and I admire that.' Then he shocked me when he said, 'I hear you have been speaking to Bobby Gould...' I was taken aback, and all I could managed was a straight, 'No'. He came straight back at me, 'Swear on your daughter's life you haven't been speaking with Bobby Gould.' I explained, I can't do that. He then knew. He told me that he had agreed £200,000 with Wimbledon and I had to go to a payphone at The Cliff training ground to ring Bobby Gould and tell him the deal was done. Fergie told me he had sympathy with my position, that I had become frustrated at not playing much and felt it was a good time for me to leave. I thought, though, 'How the hell did he know that? Has he got spies at the hotel? Does he get tip-offs from the telephonist? How on earth does he know everything that goes on when it concerns his club? Somehow he knew that Bobby Gould had made an illegal approach for me, and that I had agreed to go. He knew everything about everybody at this club. I went upstairs, collected my boots, but I left on good terms with the club and the manager."

Gibson tried his hand at coaching and management and found his old manager always willing to help. When assistant to Sanchez at Wycombe Wanderers, where the pair almost repeated their FA Cup heroics but lost 2–1 to Liverpool in a 2001 semi-final, Sir Alex was only too willing to help out. Terry told me, "He allowed us to use the training ground at The Cliff when we were travelling for matches up north. Whenever you left a message he always got back to you and helped out. I rang him and explained what we wanted, and he allowed us to use the training facilities on a Friday night whenever we were playing in the north at places such as Rochdale and Bury. He was also very helpful with a couple of loan players. When I left United for Wimbledon I couldn't stop scoring against United, and yet he was still very helpful when I went into coaching. That sums up the man. He has always been good to me. Top man."

Sir Alex's reign began with a humiliating defeat at Oxford's Manor Ground before a modest 13,545 two days after he succeeded Ron Atkinson. Several newly acquired stars had been drinking at Big Ron's farewell party the night before. Fergie was in no mood to accept excuses. He called them in for extra gym training, informing them he would put an end to United's social club. Fergie was unimpressed by Paul McGrath's midfield performance and took him off, fearful his lifestyle meant he did not have the stamina for midfield. Three games later came his first success, United beat QPR 1–0 at Old Trafford, with a free-kick from defender John Sivebaek. Sir Alex bought just over 100 players and Sivebaek was one of the first to go. The first to arrive was Viv Anderson, who replaced the Danish international. Sivebaek was sold to St. Etienne after just thirty-one games.

Anderson was lured from Arsenal for £250,000, Fergie was the motivation. Viv told me he was quite worried quitting the security of Highbury for the promise of greatness. He explained, "Bryan Robson contacted me and said they had a new manager at the club, Alex Ferguson. I had never heard of him. Robbo said that he would like to sign me. I was out of contract at Arsenal, so was entitled to talk to other clubs, and Robbo explained that he thought United would be going places under the new boss. He asked me to meet him in a hotel in Nottingham at a specific time in a specific room. I turned up a little early and wasn't in the room long when chairman Martin Edwards came in, 'Hello Viv, pleased to meet you, have you seen our manager?' Well, no I hadn't. Martin Edwards said, 'I'll go and find him, I've no idea where he could have got to, as we came in the same car.' Five minutes later in came Alex Ferguson, introduced himself, and he then asked where his chairman had got to. This must have happened four times, they kept on missing each other. I was thinking to myself, 'Hello, what have I come here for?' Initially I thought it was all very strange. But I did sign, and it was a pleasure to have played for Sir Alex."

It wasn't an auspicious start. Viv told me, "We were playing a pre-season game at Hartlepool and I can even recall the team, it was pretty impressive, Chris Turner in goal, I was at right back, Kevin Moran and Paul McGrath the centre halves, Arthur Albiston at left back, Gordon Strachan on the right wing, Norman Whiteside and Bryan Robson in centre midfield, Jesper Olsen, Brian McClair and Mark Hughes up front. We were 5–nil down at half time. The manager went berserk at half time, teacups were thrown, and he was screaming, not just at the whole team, he went along the line screaming at each and every one of us individually, the veins in his neck were massive, he was so furious. It had the desired effect. We lost 6–0!

"There was only one other time, I was in trouble with the manager. I was hauled off in our home game with Liverpool. I stormed out of the ground, and he called me into his office the next day. He told me, 'You always stay and watch the game and support the team.' I told him how annoyed and upset I was, but he told me in no uncertain terms that he wouldn't put up with it again. Other than that we never had a cross word, and when my time was up at the club, he could have insisted on a fee for me, but he let me leave on a free transfer. And he asked me to come back for European nights as he wanted me to share my experiences and knowledge with some of the young kids coming through such as Beckham, Giggs, Scholes and Butt. He thought just being in the dressing room to share a few ideas would help. It was a special place to have played, and I consider my time there special." Viv played a significant role in Fergie's new-look side until Dennis Irwin arrived from Oldham for £625,000.

Fergie bought gifted strikers, such as Eric Cantona and Robin van Persie. Rio Ferdinand observed in his podcast, *Vibe with Five*, "Fergie was great at identifying certain individuals that could win us titles. He did it with Berbatov, he did it with Tevez, he obviously did it with Cristiano, Rooney, me. But with Robin van Persie, that was one that not everyone saw as being 'that guy' who could come in and change everything. I remember the manager brought us in on the Monday and we did a video looking at a game – we very rarely did a video on a Monday. He played the video, and it just showed about fifteen clips of Van Persie making runs and us not finding him. The manager is stopping the video and saying, 'What are you thinking, what are you doing? He will win you titles, he will win you the league. Pass him the ball!' He kept going over the clips, 'Look at him running, what is wrong with you? Why are you not seeing this? Give it to him!' He was screaming at the boys. From that moment, the ball was just being zinged into him. To his feet, over the top, round the side, because they saw. Once the ball got there, the guy didn't miss. He was a killer. Unbelievable."

However, for every Keane there was a Kleberson, for every Ronaldo a Bebe. In his autobiography, Sir Alex named players that, 'Could never be left out of a Man United side' Scholes and Robson were certs in midfield, but he couldn't leave out Keane. Cantona up front, of course, but Sir Alex was torn about who to play alongside him, McClair, Hughes, Solskjaer, van Nistelrooy, Sheringham, Yorke, Cole, Rooney and van Persie. Giggs and Cristiano Ronaldo could never be left out.

Sir Alex first said of Scholes that he was too small, but he grew a few inches by the time he turned eighteen, Ferguson wrote, "When he developed into a central midfield player, he had the brain for the passing game and a talent for orchestration. He must have been a natural. I loved watching teams trying to mark him out of the game. He would take them into positions they didn't want to go to, and with a single touch would turn the ball around the corner, or feint away and hit the reverse pass. Opponents would spend a minute tracking him and then be made to appear inconsequential or even foolish. They would end up galloping back to their own box. He would destroy a marker that way." Fergie called Scholes, "Probably the best English midfielder since Bobby Charlton," elevating him above Gascoigne because of his longevity and for improving himself after he turned thirty.

Sir Alex once told his close friend Alastair Campbell, "The thing is, I have been here while all these changes have gone on, and I've managed to adapt and help players adapt. I was here before agent power, before freedom of contract, before the really big money from TV kicked in. Part of my job is to make sure these lads keep their feet on the ground. I hammer it into them that the work ethic is what got them through the door here in the first place, and they must never lose it. I say to them, 'When you're going home to your mother, you make sure she's seeing the same person she sent to me, because if you take all this fame and money the wrong way, your mother will be disappointed with you.'"

When asked whether the fame and the money change players for the worse, he responded, "Well, some footballers it might, but look at Paul Scholes, Ryan Giggs, Gary Neville, model professionals who have also handled the celebrity status well. So then the younger ones look up to them, too. You're talking about some really big characters in a top football club. And the job of the manager is to get the best out of them, for the team as a whole, and always be looking to the future as well. That must be so important in politics, too. Cantona – one of the best buys I ever made in terms of his overall impact. And that's my point, in a way. He was a great footballer. Andy Cole was a great footballer. But nobody can do it on their own. It's about the team. I can give the leadership and the direction, but the team has to gel. That means keeping them together, able to live with each other in the same room, get the best from each other."

Denis Irwin ranks as one of Fergie's all-time best buys at £625,000, guaranteed a place in his all-time team. He called him 'eight out of ten Denis.' Irwin made one error, allowing Dennis Bergkamp to score late. The press said, "Well, you'll be disappointed with Denis." Sir Alex replied, "Aye, well, he's been with me for eight or nine years and he's never made a mistake, I think we can forgive him one."

"In terms of the regrets, the 1994 team I had, the back four all seemed to grow old together, and that's a terrible thing to happen to the manager because these guys were fantastic for me. Paul Parker, Steve Bruce, Gary Pallister, Denis Irwin: Fantastic players. They gave me nine or ten years and the evidence is always on the football field. They don't see it. I see it. The problem for me is 'What do I do about it?' I managed to organise a move for them, and they did well out of it, but telling them is very, very difficult. The same when having to let young players go. The process was the youth coach and the welfare chap would come in with the player you're going to let go. The problem for me is, 'What do I do about it?' Maybe he's only seventeen, eighteen years of age. The way we'd explain it is we'd try and get him a team. We'd try and get him a club and, 'We're sorry we're having to do this.' That's terrible. That is the worst thing, having to let a young player go. All his ambitions and hopes and desires are about playing for Manchester United in front of 75,000 people and going to Wembley in a final. That's the ambition of every young kid that comes to Manchester United, and when you take that away from him, it's a sore, sore thing. So I hated that. I hated that."

Not getting Gazza was one of his biggest disappointments, edged out of it by Spurs. "He was a fabulous footballer and he would have done brilliantly here," Fergie once said of him. But there were quite a few who escaped the net, despite Fergie's best endeavours. Such was Gary Mabbutt's standing in the game at the height of his playing career, that Sir Alex tried to sign him. Gary recalls, "In 1987 I spoke with Sir Alex, well he was just plain Alex Ferguson back then, when he wanted to sign me, but I decided to stay at Spurs. I'd already been with Spurs for five years and didn't want to go. Alex was fine about it and understood why I wanted to stay with Spurs. The first time I went back to Old Trafford, right at the start of the following season, I was contacted by *The Sun* newspaper for an article about having turned down United. I said all the right things: why I didn't sign, why I wanted to stay with Spurs. It could have been a great opportunity for me, but my heart was at Spurs. The article was fine, but not the headline which read: 'United Mean Nothing To Me.' For the first time in my entire career, from the moment I walked out onto the pitch, the fans booed me from start to finish.

"After the game I spoke with Sir Alex and he was as good as gold and said that he felt that the article reflected my views and opinions accurately, but he also understood that the headline was provocative and did me no favours with the United fans. Sir Alex made sure I was able to put my point of view in the club programme for the next game, and the next time I was at Old Trafford, the fans were OK with me, no more booing. That shows you the kind of person Sir Alex is. Of course I come into contact with Sir Alex, although I wouldn't say I was a friend, put it this way I'm not on his birthday card list! But I do know him and respect him, and in particular respect what he does for so many charities. I was an Ambassador for the Prince's Trust from the very start when I was still captain of Spurs and Sir Alex often attends functions and charity events involving the Prince's Trust with Prince Charles and Camilla present. I cannot recall a single bad word between us in all the times we have met up. As for his career, I have the utmost respect for him. His career speaks for itself. He is up there with the very best there has ever been, and I have worked with some great managers in my time at Spurs, none more so than Bill Nicholson, he wasn't bad himself! What Sir Alex achieved at Manchester United is extraordinary when you consider how the club was when he first arrived there."

Paul Stewart twice had his phone ringing with Sir Alex at the other end trying to entice him to Old Trafford. The first time it was pretty audacious as Stewart was a star of the City attack, as he told me, "I scored thirty goals and had quite a few teams chasing me including Everton, Rangers, Spurs and United. Back then it was commonplace that either the manager called you or got somebody to do it for them. If they were going to spend £1.7m, a lot back then, they would want to know if you were interested rather than waste their time. Sometimes they would get one of the press lads to ring you. Really you would say yes to everyone, to find out what was what, so it was farcical really.

"I'm a United fan, so you can imagine how pleased I was when Alex Ferguson rang me. Not that I told anyone at the time I supported United, as I was playing for City! I'd have got lynched. It was an exciting time, I had 'Venners' [Terry Venables] wanting me at Spurs and Everton were really keen. I was in the manager's office and he [Mel Machin] told me City had received two bids, from Tottenham and Everton. I was fuming because I knew United had been in. It was tricky how I approached it, but I went straight to the point and asked, 'Are there only two clubs – I don't believe you.' The response was, 'Go and ask the chairman.' The chairman's office was next to the manager's office in the old Maine Road ground, so I went straight into see Peter Swales. I told him, 'The manager says only two clubs are in for me. There are more than two and I know it.' Swales replied, 'If the other club is who I think you are talking about, you are going there over my dead body.' I told Swales, 'You are lying to me then as you know other clubs are in for me,' and I turned round, walked out and slammed the door.' I ended up signing for Tottenham.

"Fast forward and I am leaving Spurs to sign for Liverpool, and they were offering me fantastic wages. Fergie again came in for me again, but his salaries were capped as no one could go above Bryan Robson who was their highest paid player, whereas Liverpool offered me twice the money that Robbo was on. It didn't work out at Liverpool where I was played in midfield, and I thought my career was going downhill. Now Swales wanted to bring me back to City and a deal was agreed, but manager at the time at Anfield was Graeme Souness who said to me, 'If you want to f****** leave this club you will have to forgo your signing on fee.' At the time there was talk of Liverpool getting rid of Souness but would have to give him a £750,000 pay off, so I said to him, 'I'll forgo my signing on fee, if you forgo your £750,000 f****** pay off.' I was consigned to train with the kids. But I didn't return to City as I had called Swales a 'lying bastard', so I joined Peter Reid at Sunderland."

Darren Anderton turned down a dream move to Old Trafford despite a tempting personal call from Sir Alex, but he then got a call from his chairman Alan Sugar to persuade him to sign a new contract. Anderton scored the goal of his England career, a half-volley in the 90th minute to secure a 3–3 draw with Sweden at Elland Road, and then first became aware of interest from Sir Alex, as after that game Gary Pallister asked over a game of snooker back at the team hotel whether he fancied a move to United and suggested he gave Sir Alex his number.

Ferguson seemed to be 'in the know' about players contracts and discovered a release clause in Anderton's contract: any club bidding £4m activated that clause. Fergie wanted Anderton to replace Andrei Kanchelskis. Sir Alex called Anderton, his brother shocked when he answered the phone, but the next day he saw Sir Alan Sugar who didn't let him leave his house without signing a new contract to replace that clause. Klinsmann, Popescu and Barmby all wanted to leave and Sir Alan wanted to make sure he didn't lose Anderton to United as well and gave him 'a ridiculous contract.' Equally, Sir Alex needed Anderton, with Hughes, Kanchelskis and Ince on their way out.

When I caught up with Darren in the States I asked him exactly what Sir Alex said to him in that phone call? Darren texted me the answer, "He just said he'd like to sign me as he'd had a problem with Kanchelskis. He asked me to come up there and have a look around and have a chat. I was open to that but the next day Alan Sugar called me to his house and offered me a new contract and I signed it." Anderton's snub didn't go down well, as their paths crossed not too long after and he got a very frosty reception. Darren told me, "When I saw Fergie at Spurs a few months later it was pretty obvious he wasn't best pleased with me and didn't really respond when I said, 'Hello' to him in passing." I imagined it was a pretty grim Fergie stare? "Ha ha, yeah a little one."

Darren wasn't the only winger who got away. Arjen Robben wanted to join United after dining with Fergie in Manchester and looking round the training ground but United dallied so PSV Eindhoven sold him to Chelsea for a bargain £12m. Robben said, "Had Manchester United offered me a deal straight after I met them, I would have signed there. But it didn't happen and I have got no regrets."

Ferguson rejected the chance to bring Ronaldo to United in 1996. At the time, the Brazilian striker was in the middle of his one and only season with Barcelona. Fergie was offered the chance to pay the player's buyout clause and would sign Teddy Sheringham the following summer after Cantona retired. But Ferguson decided not to pursue the deal for Ronaldo, as he was suspicious of Ronaldo's agent. In 2003, Ronaldo scored a hat-trick at Old Trafford to knock Manchester United out of the Champions League. United supporters gave him a standing ovation.

One of the famous Allen family, the player and manager they called Mad Dog would never have turned down Sir Alex. Unfortunately, he never quite got the offer that he couldn't refuse. Martin tells me, "I only met Sir Alex once. It was a Tuesday night at the Baseball Ground during half time at a Derby County game. I was in the directors' lounge with my father, as I had been invited up there by the then Derby County manager Arthur Cox with a view to signing for the club. The fee had been agreed with QPR and my manager there Trevor Francis. A few days before in a newspaper a small paragraph said that United were interested in the QPR midfielder, Martin Allen, so somebody told us, and naturally we were intrigued as we had heard nothing about it. When I told my dad, who was also my agent, what I had heard about the newspaper report he told me, 'If he comes in for you, you have to sign for Manchester United.' I told my dad I hadn't heard anything, but he said, 'If Alex Ferguson is in for you, he will find you, don't worry about that.' Anyway, we heard nothing, so we drove up to Derby County to watch the match and to make up our minds about a move there.

"At half time we went into the tearoom to get ourselves a nice cuppa, and in the directors' lounge it was all lovely china teacups and saucers with lovely red roses on them, all very posh. Oh my God, the next in the queue for the tea was... Sir Alex Ferguson. He said, 'Good evening, Martin, hello, Mr Allen,' he was very polite especially to my dad. I said to him, 'If you don't mind me asking, we saw something in the newspaper that you wanted to sign me.' We wanted to clear up whether there was anything in it, and there was the man himself. He replied, 'Aye, son, I like you as a player, but when I asked for you, they were asking too much money for you, as I was thinking of you as part of the squad.' So I asked him, 'So you wouldn't go up to the asking price?' He didn't actually answer that, but said, 'I told Arthur Cox to sign you.' 'Oh really...' I replied. Next day I signed for West Ham.

"At the time I had a very young family, and really didn't want to move away from the grandparents and the family. While driving up to Derby to see the game, it felt like an awful long way from home, and I wanted to stay down south, especially when West Ham came in for me. I was never really a fan of a club as a kid because from twelve, thirteen, fourteen I was at a lot of different clubs watching different teams, but because of the Allen family links to West Ham and coming from Essex, I had to sign for West Ham, there was no doubt about it."

Most synonymous with rejecting Sir Alex is Alan Shearer. Big Al was twice offered the chance of a move to Old Trafford. Sir Alex initially approached him before he opted for a switch to Blackburn, then he missed out once again when Shearer joined Newcastle United. Shearer spoke with Magpies manager Kevin Keegan and Sir Alex but opted to sign for his home-town club in a record £15m deal. Shearer met them both on the same day in a house in Cheshire, Keegan in the morning, the Newcastle contingent leaving as the United contingent came in. Shearer even demanded to take the penalties at Old Trafford ahead of Cantona in his talks with Fergie! Shearer rang Ferguson to inform him of his decision, but he never got a call back!

Now as one of the country's top TV pundits, I caught up with Big Al to give an assessment of Sir Alex's career. I asked him to describe Sir Alex's achievements. He laughed: "Which word would you like... spectacular, amazing... I could go on. His achievements were ridiculously good, that's the only way to put, ridiculously good. Anyone who sets out in their career to do whatever it takes to reach the top, well, no one could have done it better than Sir Alex. Has there been anyone who has done better? I don't think so. What he has achieved over such a long period of time stands him apart from anyone else. He is unique, a very, very special list of achievements. Would he have achieved even more if I had signed for him? Who knows? What I do know is that he has no regrets as he won so much without me, and I for sure don't have any regrets. He has been hugely successful and yeah, maybe I might have helped him win more trophies. We shall never know, but look, he won enough. We have talked about this more recently when we have met up, and we have had a laugh and a joke about it, and he's even presented me with a couple of awards. He certainly hasn't said much to me about my decision, although maybe he had a few quiet words to himself at the time!"

Another big name to not go to Manchester United was England winger John Barnes. In Ferguson's autobiography, he suggested that Dave Bassett, who succeeded Graham Taylor as Watford manager at the end of the 1986/87 season, had offered the United manager the chance to sign Barnes. The winger, though, reveals that at no time did Sir Alex contact him. Barnes tells me, "There were plenty of rumours that Manchester United wanted to sign me from Watford at the time, and those rumours have never gone away. The story I had heard was that Sir Alex contacted Graham Taylor who told him that I had already made up my mind to go to Liverpool, and that was the end of it. Liverpool had come in for me in January and then Graham Taylor agreed terms of £900,000 but said I couldn't go until the summer as he wanted to keep me until the end of the season."

Bassett took over from Taylor, but Barnes never played for the new boss as he was off to Anfield, without ever being approached by Sir Alex. He added, "Maybe Fergie asked Graham Taylor about me, but it must have started and ended there." Barnes, though, did meet up with Sir Alex much later. He explained, "I saw him a few times at the races, since he retired, but he never mentioned anything to me about trying to sign me, and I certainly didn't want to insult him by asking whether or not he ever did."

Barnes also worked alongside Sir Alex on ITV. He explains, "I have worked with Alex and discovered that people's perceptions of him are wrong. He is actually a very easy-going kind of guy. You will see him leaving the ground and stopping to say hello to the crowd. He has time for everyone. He is a genuine person, even though he doesn't come across like that because of his image on TV." John has nothing but respect and admiration for Sir Alex's achievements, describing them as "Incredible." He continues, "When you talk about dynasties in football, there was clearly one built at Liverpool and one was under way from Sir Matt's time at Old Trafford. But the real dynasty at Manchester United has been under construction since Alex Ferguson came along. To create something that will last, it cannot materialise overnight. Alex Ferguson was given that opportunity to develop a dynasty.

"He was incredible at Aberdeen, but even more incredible at Old Trafford. And how he did it is a lesson for all clubs. He wasn't an instant hit and took three or four years before he became successful, but he was the right man for the job, and the board had the foresight to stick by him despite his struggles to change the perception and culture at the club. The culture back in those days wasn't confined to United, we also had it at Liverpool, and it was a culture of drinking as part of the socialising, bonding, you might call it, that went on in those days. Under Bill Shankly you could do what you wanted providing you came in and were able to train to your optimum and play the same way. Senior players like Kenny Dalglish, Graeme

Souness and Alan Hansen understood how it worked, they knew their responsibilities to the club and to their team.

"Sir Alex inherited that drinking culture epitomised in players who had problems such as Paul McGrath, but Sir Alex was a disciplinarian and was brought up in an environment where the senior players set an example that the younger players followed He struggled at first to change that culture, but it took a big character like Sir Alex to get to grips with something that had been inbuilt within the game at that time. He knew there had to be radical change within the club as he had some exceptional young boys coming through such as Beckham and Giggs and he did not want them to do what they could see the senior players doing. He was determined to keep those gifted kids on the straight and narrow and it was hard at first to change that culture.

"But over a period of time, the general culture in the game was changing, with the arrival of Arsene Wenger and the new methods and diet he brought with him, creating a dynasty at Arsenal, the way Fergie was at United, and to be fair Kenny Dalglish was someone who had similar principles and was not only successful at Liverpool but also at Blackburn. Guys like Giggs and Beckham knew how to party, but it was within limits. There was no more excessive alcohol, there was a new far more professional approach under Fergie. No one was saying they never had a drink, but they were living their lives outside of football correctly. When it came to winning titles, the top players in their day at Liverpool knew you had to hit your peak in the run in around March and April, and it was the same at United.

"You would have to put Fergie right up there with the very best, if not the best of all time." Barnes elaborates, "At Liverpool there is always now talk about Jurgen Klopp and

Bob Paisley versus Bill Shankly. For me Shankly would always be the no. 1. Whatever Bob Paisley did, and he won more trophies than Shanks, it was Bill Shankly who started the revolution. But you would also put Wenger right up there, so too Kenny Dalglish. However, there is so little to divide such momentous managerial icons. In fact, I won't give you my one to three, I don't actually subscribe to putting them into that kind of category. Suffice to say that they would all be in my top five, and I don't think it matters in which order."

Emmanuel Petit, who won the double at Arsenal in 1998, left England for the Nou Camp in 2000, but after an unhappy time with Barca, he wanted to return to English football. He got a call from Sir Alex. He says, "During that bad period at Barcelona, Sir Alex Ferguson called me twice and wanted me to join Manchester United. Arsene Wenger also called me because he wanted me back at Arsenal. But Claudio Ranieri had just taken over at Chelsea and after a call with me, he came to visit me in Barcelona. Three managers had called me from three big clubs in England, but only one took a plane to come and see me. I really liked talking to Alex Ferguson, and I love the way Arsene tried to convince me to come back to Arsenal because he told me he'd made a mistake." Six months after his wife told him she wanted out of London, she wanted to return to the capital.

Fergie made bids for Gabriel Batistuta and Patrick Kluivert, but eventually paid a club record £12.6m for Dwight Yorke as a summer spree which led to the treble began with the signing of Jaap Stam for a world record for a defender, £10.75m. Selling Stam was controversial, and Fergie admitted he made a big mistake. Stam's hasty exit was due to Fergie's anger at revelations in Stam's autobiography claiming Fergie tapped him up. Sir Alex also felt the money on offer from Lazio was too much to resist, £16.5m. Stam's United career was brought to an end in a meeting with Fergie in the forecourt of a petrol station in Manchester. In his *Head to Head* autobiography, Stam said that his manager initially told him he wasn't worried about the content of his book, but he reported at 8.00am to resolve the matter. Stam wrote, "I said, 'You know what's in the book – nothing bad' but he maintained that he wasn't happy. I was left out for a game against Blackburn. On the day, he called me to say I wasn't in his squad because of the book hassle. He felt it might calm down if I wasn't playing. We had a few conversations, although none of them were really satisfactory. A bit later that week, I was driving home from training when my agent phoned, telling me I'd been sold. I was like, 'What?!' He said, 'Yeah, they'll contact you in a minute.'

"Moments later, Ferguson called me and asked where I was. We lived in the same area, and he told me to wait for him so that we could have a chat. I pulled into a petrol station near a shopping centre and he met me there. When he arrived, he got in my car and told me that the club had accepted an offer from Lazio. Within twenty-four hours, I'd gone to Rome and joined Lazio." Stam later returned to Old Trafford in the FA Cup as manager of Reading. The fans gave him a rousing reception. His song 'Yip Jaap Stam is a Big Dutch Man" rang out in his honour.

Brian McClair was one of Fergie's favourites, a snip at £850,000 in July 1987 when Fergie pinched him from Celtic. Henrik Larsson had signed in the 2007 January window on a short-term loan from Helsingborgs as cover for the injured Louis Saha, managing thirteen games and scoring three times. Ferguson wrote in his autobiography, "For a man of thirty-five years of age, his receptiveness to information on the coaching side was amazing. At every session he was rapt. He wanted to listen to Carlos [Queiroz] and the tactics lectures. He was into every nuance of what we did. In his last game, we were winning 2–1 and Henrik went back to play in midfield and ran his balls off. On his return to the dressing room, all the players stood up and applauded him, and the staff joined in." Larsson is quoted as saying, "I learned a lot from Sir Alex and the way he was with players. It didn't matter if you were younger or older, if you weren't doing your job, you were told. There was a huge respect from the players, obviously. He was absolutely fantastic towards me and my family."

A transfer list from 2004 published on social media years after Ferguson retired contains players categorised by position and value: Luke Chadwick, Michael Stewart, Nicky Butt and Diego Forlan listed in the 'excess' section. The section on 'youth potential' names Kieran Richardson, Mads Timm, Phil Bardsley and Chris Eagles. Transfer targets after losing the title to Arsenal: central defenders, Gabriel Heinze, Philippe Mexes, Vincent Kompany, Gerard Pique and only one forward, Alan Smith. United signed Heinze, Pique and Smith. In 2006 Fergie signed a leader at centre half, Nemanja Vidic from Spartak Moscow, and United won three titles from 2007 and the Champions League in 2008.

Ole Gunnar Solskjaer received a message from Sir Alex before his first game. "I got a text from the manager who said, 'Pick your team and sleep well.' I sent him the players I was picking and I just got a message back, 'That'll do the job.'" United won 5–1 at Cardiff. Fergie commented on the improvement under Solskjaer, "It's not an easy road to get back into challenging for the league. It's a difficult league these days." He spotted Ole's attention to detail at an early stage at Old Trafford as he explained, "Ole used to take down all the training sessions, and as a sub – and he was sub many times, as you know – he would watch the game all the time. Sometimes subs will sit and look round the stadium and chat to each other. Not him. Solskjaer was always on the game."

Instead of a blasting when he annoyed Fergie, Ole got his first break into coaching! Ole was parking up at the training ground as the manager was coming out. Fergie asked, "How are you, son?"

"Not great," replied Solskjaer. "I need another operation. I'm not going to do it, I need to retire." Fergie responded, "Well don't worry, son, you've had a fantastic career, your family must be so proud. Your last season was fantastic. Why don't you coach my forwards? Go home for a few weeks and come back when you're ready." Ole coached Ronaldo, Rooney and Tevez and was so proud whenever Cristiano or Rooney scored through the defender's legs, Ole says, "I nudge my son Noah and say, 'Your dad taught them that.'"

One of the Class of '92 was Nicky Butt, in United's team for twelve of Sir Alex's twenty-seven years in charge. Few know Sir Alex better. Nicky once described Sir Alex as a "God of the club." Now, in this book to commemorate Sir Alex's 80th year, he describes the incredible influence Sir Alex extended far beyond the pitch. Nicky tells me, "Sir Alex was a phenomenal man-manager, but also immensely forward thinking, not like the stereotype, old-school manager he is often portrayed as, quite different in fact. He brought in sports science and different collaborations. Never one to be satisfied with his success he brought in different people, different coaches all the way through his career. Add to that a relentless work ethic which he possessed and instilled in everyone around him.

"I have known him since I first arrived at the club at the age of fourteen, and it was astounding how much interest he took in the young players, even at that early age. He knew the names of our parents and our siblings. He became a massive influence on us as young men. He could have been our teacher, scout leader, he was a father figure, a huge influence on our young lives, keeping us young men on the straight and narrow, how to conduct ourselves. Sometimes when we fell off the straight and narrow he would put you back on it, show you how to behave.

"He treated everyone with respect whether it was the kit man, the laundry lady, the receptionist, he believed in creating one big family. Looking back, you can appreciate the massive influence he had, and which is still there. By the time we were seventeen, whenever you had a problem, or made a mistake, he was the one to go to, to sort it out for you. He helped us through those times, as a second father, looking after your best interests, a confidante you could trust with your problems, and trust to be on your side. He was someone you could look to. Growing up as young men going out in Manchester city centre there are bound to be issues from time to time. Once in the first team at the age of nineteen, twenty, it was all about football talk, match preparation, reflection on the games, but there were times when you needed the manager's help and then you would see a different side to him. He knew his young players were going through different life experiences and he was there to help you. He even shows that to this day, he is someone you can call for advice and help, and he was straight forward with you, no bullshit. I probably talk to him once a week, and often to bounce things off him.

"Yes, there have been plenty of times I'd see the hairdryer. The first time when I was fifteen we played Blackburn in a youth cup tie, and I tried something to show how good I was and it didn't work, and he gave me a roasting. I've seen many others, many times, on the end of it in the dressing room. But it was not personal, or out of order. When it all settled down and you had time to think about these episodes you realise that it was actually done in the right way, for the right reasons. He didn't stand any fools." As for Nicky's assessment, "I don't think there are too many, if any, you could put next to him to compare. He was Manchester United's super-boss and I don't think we shall see the like of him again the way he put seven or eight great teams together, how he changed it each time, different teams, different leaders, and how he moved with the times to achieve that. He was a genius in the way he did that. So many managers are stuck in their ways, stubbornly refusing to change. Not him. Despite being massively successful, he was still prepared to change, never prepared to stand still, or allow players to stay when he knew it was time to move them on. He kept things fresh. He took management to different heights."

That Mark Goal

History tells us that only a late goal from young striker Mark Robins saved Sir Alex, who was still plain Alex Ferguson back then, from an ignominious exit from Old Trafford. It is often cited Mark's goal saved Sir Alex from the sack as the United board wavered on whether they had given him long enough. When Ferguson landed the United job, "He was in awe of the place when he first came down, no question" according to Norman Whiteside. "He used to come to us in training and say, 'Big place this, big place.'" Maybe it was too big for him, when during a 2–1 home defeat to lowly Crystal Palace, a banner was unfurled which read, 'Three years of excuses and it's still crap – ta-ra, Fergie.' Ferguson recognised it was a low point. "Every time somebody looks at me, I feel I have betrayed United," he said at the time.

'That' Robins goal set them on their way to a vital cup run. But did Robins' goal save his manager? "I've no clue, though, if that was actually the case, no clue to this day, thirty-one years later", reflected the man himself currently the Coventry City manager. Fergie was famously on the brink when Robins headed in Mark Hughes' cross in the third-round tie at Nottingham Forest. United went on to win the FA Cup with Robins scoring against Newcastle and then Oldham in the semi-finals to enable his manager to lift his first silverware before going on to greatness. "How many times have I been asked about that goal? I have no idea, but put it this way, I've lost count."

Robins didn't object to me asking it again, and he was more than happy to recount it in graphic detail. "Whatever the significance of that goal, I was just happy to have scored it at the time, and looking back now, yet again, I didn't look at it in the way it has been portrayed as potentially the goal that saved the manager, I didn't know that at the time, and to be fair, don't know that even now. I do know it was an important goal on the day I scored it, and I was very happy to have scored. I recall that the lads were up for the tie. We stayed overnight, it was a Sunday match, live on BBC. I had only just broken into the first team, and only then because of some injuries, in fact so many injuries that Brian McClair played in midfield in the absence of Bryan Robson. I was so pleased, though, whatever the circumstances, to have been picked for the starting line-up. I was up front alongside Mark Hughes. But it was a tough looking tie, against a Brian Clough side packed with great players, like Neil Webb, Stuart Pearce and Nigel Clough. They were a top team at the time with outstanding players, it was a huge game, and we found it difficult physically but also because of the quality they possessed.

"Mark Hughes took a lot of stick, but he took a lot of weight from myself up front, and then came the moment... Lee Martin, on the left, hit a lovely cross with the outside of his right foot, because of the pitch the ball sat up nicely for him to strike it. The cross didn't have a great deal of pace, but I headed it back from where it came from. Normally I would have flicked that ball but didn't have much choice as I was pushed in the back by Stuart Pearce which took me onto the ball. I scored only my second goal for the team, and we won the game. For me, and I am sure, the rest of the team, it was a chance to move on to to Edgar Street and play Hereford in the next round, which we did on an horrific pitch. But that win against Forest gave us belief, it raised our confidence levels that we could pick up results despite our recent torrid spell."

Robins enjoyed a good relationship with Fergie. "Every young player benefited from Sir Alex, and the same can be said of myself. I owe him a lot. I scored a load of goals in the youth teams, fifty goals a season for three seasons, and we had a manager that stood by the young players coming through. In my case, though, I had to wait eighteen months before I got my first goal, which came at Plough Lane against Wimbledon, as I was in an out of the team. I got the second for United to give us a 2–2 draw, a good enough result, and my first goal as well. I've taken a lot of what I learned back then into my managerial career. I didn't get the so-called hairdryer treatment as such but got my fair share of rebukes if they were needed, but that was all part of growing up. For the manager, he saw the bigger picture. For him, it was all about the team, and he had a lot of impressionable young lads, and he wanted to make the right impression on us. Whatever he said to us, he never dwelt on things, he didn't hold a grudge, and got on with it. But, equally, you knew you only had so many 'lives' and couldn't push your luck too far. That was the Manchester United culture he wanted to build, and that is what he achieved. He was making sure the young lads were brought up in the right way."

After Hereford, United went to Newcastle and won 3–2, and Mark scored again. Then The Red Devils beat Sheffield United 1–0 at Bramall Lane, followed by two epic semifinals against Oldham, drawing 3–3 and then Mark scored the winner in the replay at Maine Road, which took their manager to Wembley. For Robins, his winning goal in the Cup semi-final against Oldham seemed far more important than the one against Forest. But it didn't guarantee him a place in the final. He was a sub. There were only two subs in those days. He got on in the first game but not in the replay because United were soon 1-0 up and Fergie shored up defence. United won the FA Cup and then the European Cup Winners' Cup followed, with Mark on the bench in the final against Barcelona in Rotterdam.

Joe Royle has a special bond with Sir Alex. Fergie has nothing but admiration for the former England centre-forward. That was clear enough when Sir Alex penned the Foreword to his autobiography. Despite Sir Alex's record-busting trophy-laden career, the FA Cup semi-final against Joe's Oldham remains a defining moment. Sir Alex and Joe remain close to this day, and Sir Alex mentioned in his Foreword Joe's ability to spot free transfers and bargain buys reminded him of his early managerial days with East Stirlingshire when he picked up his first signing, George Adams, for the princely sum of £100. Sir Alex reflected, "I can honestly say that our FA Cup semi-final meeting with Oldham Athletic in 1990 remains one of my enduring memories. Oldham was the small-town team who had grabbed the imagination of the football world. Their manager was Joe Royle. And what a manager! Joe's Second Division – pre-Premier League, of course – team of free transfer and bargain buys produced a footballing miracle that season by reaching the Littlewoods Cup final after a string of giant-killing feats that thrilled not only their own disbelieving public but also, a disbelieving nationwide audience. They also gave my United team a hell of a fright before we finally beat them then 2-1 in a replay at Maine Road."

In the replay United trailed, then equalised but only a late Robins goal took United through to the final. Sir Alex had to drop his captain Bryan Robson back into defence to hold on. Joe tells me, "When Sir Alex first came down from Scotland to Manchester, one of the first things he did was to ring round the local managers, to get to know them, and from the very start we had a fine relationship, we got on well, and still do. In fact he recommended me to take over as manager at Aberdeen when I was still manager of little Oldham. He still has plenty of sway at Aberdeen, he was still a big part of Aberdeen, and I was very much appreciative of how highly he must have rated me to do that. Of course we played United in those two cup semi-finals, and although he beat us in the replay he was gracious enough to praise our performances before they went on to beat Crystal Palace in the final."

When Joe took little Oldham to the Premier League, Fergie wanted to show how much he thought of Royle's achievement. Joe tells me, "He came to our promotion celebration party, which shows you what the man was about." Sir Alex continued in the Foreword, "Yet, for me, the most impressive aspect of Joe Royle, the football manager, is the way he has clung to his balanced perspective on life, and significantly, kept his sense of humour. I have known so many managers whose humour has drained away over the years, leaving them unrecognisable as the same person who set out in the job. That hasn't happened to Joe." Royle also likes to recall how he set Sir Alex on the path to glory by helping to convince him to purchase Denis Irwin from his club. He explains, "We talked a lot back then, and still see quite a bit of each other now, but he wanted to know about Denis Irwin before he bought him, so he asked me. He had had thirteen reports on him, and they were all top reports all saying how good he was, but he still wanted my opinion. I told him, 'Alex, I have no doubt you are buying him as cover, but, believe me, it won't be long before he will be your first choice, and he will be the best buy you will ever make."

Sir Alex recalls, "He left behind a legacy of twelve truly remarkable years at Boundary Park, a period in which he turned so many players into top-class professionals, including free-transfer full back Denis Irwin, for whom United paid £625,000. Denis ranks amongst the best buys I ever made."

When Sir Alex took over from the late Jock Stein as manager of Scotland, one of the first managers to call him was Joe, "Joe rang me and as good as demanded that I pick his goalkeeper Andy Goram." Sir Alex rang Jimmy Conway of Bolton and asked him to watch Goram in the next three games, and Sir Alex was impressed that Royle's judgement was spot on and he gave the goalkeeper his debut against Romania. When Royle moved on to Everton, his team beat Sir Alex's United in the 1995 FA Cup Final. Joe says, "Not so long-ago Peter Reid and I visited Sir Alex at his home, rather his palace, and once again we talked football and enjoyed his company."

On reflection, the entire Ferguson success story still hinged on the board keeping their nerve. Ferguson once explained, "Until I first won the League with United, it was like an albatross around my neck, and that applied to everyone else who'd managed the club since Sir Matt Busby. And after losing it last year, it was everything to us to prove this season that we were the best team in the country. The younger players in the side, like David Beckham, had lost something, which was very serious to them. He was used to winning everything since coming through the youth ranks. What happened to us last season has a lot to do with the determination we have shown this season. Their attitude was one of, 'We've got to get to grips with the situation – we can't let that happen again.'"

Sir Bobby Charlton explains why they stuck with Ferguson, "You can tell when something is right. You don't have to be a great soothsayer when you can see that someone can do a good job. Everybody would prefer success to come immediately, but it doesn't happen that way, and we could see the potential. We were quite certain he was the correct man for the job. What happened with Ferguson should be a good example to others. Too many clubs don't give their managers the backing they deserve. Sometimes the crowd prove to be too influential in calling for a manager to go. There were never any personality clashes here at Old Trafford between the board and the manager – we just knew we had the right man. When he arrived he said that to build the team he wanted it would take between three and four years. He would need to wait for contracts to expire to let players go and to acquire the ones he wanted. He has been proved right in that.

"One thing sets him aside from most of his contemporaries. He has achieved success consistently. In the modern game, managers can become casualties of even their own success because after three or four years they have to move on as their players don't seem to listen to them anymore. But Alex is not afraid to take on that challenge. A mark of his success is that everybody wants to play for him. He has earned their respect. Even the youngsters want to come to Manchester United because they know the manager's philosophy is that if they are good enough then they will get a game irrespective of their age. He gives them hope and confidence. Confidence goes right through the club. He has created success at every level of the club and that all reflects in the glory years he has brought to it.

"From the moment he arrived to take charge of the team he has had this enthusiasm for the game. He is quite prepared to travel 300 miles, through the night if necessary, if he thinks there is a player he needs to watch before thinking about signing him, even if it is a young player. He will jump in his car at any time to cover a match anywhere if he thinks it will be worthwhile, with one motive – to bring success to his team."

Sir Bobby was convinced Fergie was the only man capable of lifting the club out of crisis following the failure of five previous managers to win the championship. "He was desperate for the job – he couldn't wait. Managing Manchester United was the ultimate challenge. There was no fear in him. No worry that having become such a big name in Scotland it would all go wrong down here. I had persuaded the club to talk to Alex and I'm proud of that. I've always believed he would crack it here. But the credit only goes to one person – Alex Ferguson. It was bound to take him time to get things moving in the way he wanted. But once he cracked it with his first trophy there was never going to be any stopping him. I always believed that.

"Personally, I never had any doubts about what Alex could achieve with us. By the time we won at Wembley in 1990 I reckon he was bang on course. I knew people had been calling for his head but as a board of directors we decided that when we appointed Alex we were going to give him the time he needed no matter what. He has shown incredible self-belief, great personal resilience, tactical awareness – and just would not let himself be deflected."

Sir Bobby watched with enormous pride for 'his' club as Manchester United reaped the rewards of Sir Alex's master plan that Sir Bobby confessed was, "something that took quite some time to come together." He elaborated, "We set the standard for others to follow. Everything was in place. We have shown the value of having faith in your manager. You have to be positive. We had the right man, so we gave him the time he needed. Alex has helped lead a revolution at Old Trafford and he was given the backing to do it. He got down to business right away, sometimes working twenty hours a day. There was no question of him relaxing and delegating responsibility. In fact, the only problem was calming him down, making him take a break. That was just about impossible.

"He is an enthusiast, and he's always talking about the game. He knows every player at every club. He has earned his success. He's given us exciting times and an exciting team, and that's precisely what we wanted at Manchester United."

How Sir Alex 'Sold' United

Sir Alex turned on the charm offensive when it came to recruiting key players. His big sell was the personal touch, the way he adored everything connected to the club came across in such a subtle, yet infectious, way.

Paul Parker is a big Spurs fan and had the opportunity to sign for his boyhood love when he met Terry Venables and his dream move was almost sealed – until he got the call to go north. Paul's account of how he was lured to Old Trafford by Sir Alex, the man he still calls The Boss to this day, perfectly illustrates the manager's methods. Paul tells me, "I'm a Spurs supporter, an Essex boy, played my football in Rainham and Dagenham areas, and always had a close relationship with Spurs and would have loved to played for them, and in fact, had the big chance to do just that when I met Terry Venables to discuss a transfer to the club. I met Terry at the Royal Lancaster Hotel in central London to discuss my move to Spurs and I told him that I really wanted to sign for Spurs and that was going to be it, unless I had a call from their director Maurice Watkins at Manchester United which I was promised I would get before I made up my mind. I told Terry that if I got that call I would have to listen to what they had to say. That call arrived and Terry was great about it, and actually told me, 'You have to be respectful, and go and listen to what they have to say.' Then Terry shrugged his shoulders and added, 'but if you do go up there, you won't be coming back!' He was right."

Paul describes how Sir Alex made it so enticing you wouldn't want to sign for any other club. "When I walked into the room at Old Trafford to discuss things, there was their chairman Martin Edwards, Maurice Watkins, and Sir Alex. They all got up and we all shook hands, and almost immediately Sir Alex told me that he was going to walk me around the side of the pitch. I had played at Old Trafford before, but probably no more than three or four times, and wondered what this was all about because I knew Old Trafford, or at least I thought I did. But when Sir Alex walked me around the perimeter of the pitch I saw Old Trafford and Manchester United in a different light to the one I remembered when I was running out onto that pitch to play.

"As we walked and talked he would tell me about every part of the ground and point it out to me, how many fans were in which sections, what type of fans. He'd say those fans there, they are not communicating with the players, they might as well be watching the grass grow, and there, they are ones who have travelled from all over the world, but there, they are the fans who will get the players going, that's the part where all the famous people sit, but so many people want to come to this stadium, so many can't get a ticket, or live so far away they can't get to the stadium. There are some who come from abroad and want a tour of the stadium, museum, spend their entire day here at this football club, it means so much to so many millions of people all over the world. He knew every inch of the place and talked about it in such reverential terms that he didn't need to talk football or sell the football to me, you just took it all in and knew this was the place to play your football. He never once mentioned anything about me signing or going to be here, not once. But in the fifteen to twenty minutes we spent walking around the pitch he had sold the football club to me, and you knew you wouldn't want to be playing anywhere else. As much as I loved my time at QPR, as much as I wanted to play for Tottenham being a lifelong fan, and having watched them so many times, it was clear that Old Trafford was the place to be.

"I always knew how much people respected him, but how much he respected being manager of Manchester United. He looked upon that club as part of his family and held it as dear to him. He knew every bit of that football club, he loved being in charge of it, and being embroiled in every aspect of it, and you felt the only way he would be gone from this club, was when he was gone! Sir Alex was very much his own person, but managers like Sir Alex are extinct from the modern game at the top level, they are no longer the manager, they are the coach, but clubs still need 'managers' from the lower half of the Championship and below all the way to the National league; there you manage the players and also manage the club.

"Sir Alex's forte was to ensure that all the players had no issues when it came round to match days. To that end he wanted to be proactive, he wanted to know what the issues were before they became issues or someone was knocking on his door telling him about them, he wanted to know beforehand. He didn't want any surprises, he wanted to be on top of any situation. He believed in you, believed in his players and would defend them to the hilt, but could only defend them if he knew in advance their problems. If he had any issues with you he would let you know collectively and often on an individual basis. But good, bad or indifferent, whatever the level of your problem, he wanted to know what it was before someone told him. Once he was on top of situations he would be the first to want to protect you, and in return he wanted you to believe in him."

Even mild-mannered Paul got the 'hairdryer.' "It was my first season and I really blame Steve Bruce for it. He said something to me and it stuck in my head, and as a young player, it was something that should have stayed inside my head but didn't. It was during a training session. We were doing a session we often did, with players in two boxes, one box containing the young players like Beckham, the Neville brothers, Butt, Scholes and Giggs, and the other box the senior players, although Giggs was a regular by this time, he still liked to be with his contemporaries, and even changed with them in their dressing room at The Cliff, he never forgot where he came from. On the odd occasion The Boss would join in, when you went into one box, first touch, and out and then on rotation. The Boss ended up in the middle and we would try to keep in as long as possible. I did something out of the ordinary, I pulled something out of my locker I didn't think I had – I nutmegged The Boss! Then I made a big song and dance about it, and the other players joined it. We all thought it was great fun. The Boss didn't. He came over right into my face, calling me all the names under the sun. I recalled what Steve Bruce had said to me and what he had called The Boss, after a very famous Scottish actor, and although you knew, you really did know, that if you said something to him when he was sounding off you were taking your life into your own hands. But I said, 'Oh come on, Taggart...'

"Oh my God, the next five seconds seemed like five hours. One thing he said, I wouldn't even care to repeat, but I didn't really take offence, it was water off a duck's back, but you could sense the other players in the background in complete shock but holding their shoulders in to try to hold back the laughter. I might as well have called his mother out. It was a pretty scary moment, I don't think even the players used to his hairdryer rants had witnessed anything quite like it even at half-time or after a game. It is pointless trying to say anything once he has launched into his tirade, all you succeed in doing is getting tongue-tied, and he's not listening anyway when he's screaming at you and adding some swearing as he gets louder and louder, you just can't compete. So, it's best to step aside and come back to see him another time when it's possible to actually talk to him.

"I thought to myself 'what the f*** have I done?' I spent the rest of that training session wondering if it was actually my last. It was my first season and already he wasn't very happy with me, although, to be fair, I didn't really help myself by what I did and said. But The Boss didn't like Londoners at the best of times, he called everybody Cockneys no matter what part of the south of the country they came from. I didn't have the heart to try to explain the term Cockney and that it was from a specific area of London, and in any case, I came from Essex.

"It was such a scary experience, I was still scared to go in the next day training, and when I did it felt as though I was walking into the headmaster's office to receive six of the best. I thought it was going to take a while to regain my confidence, and I thought the best thing to do was to stay out of his way in the hope he wouldn't see me. I had this dread that he would send me packing the next time he spotted me. I kept thinking as I went back to training, 'Why did I do that?' I was still a newbie, it was just my first season, what was I thinking? I was wrong to have worried. I found out that he might explode from time to time, but he doesn't bear grudges.

"If you piped up and told him you disagreed with something, he would just say, 'Come and see me tomorrow morning at The Cliff.' I'd ask what time and he would say I get to The Cliff at 7.00am, I'll see you at five past. You'd walk into his office and he would be on a swivel chair which he would swivel around to show you he had a panoramic view of the training pitch, he wanted to let you know that you could never hide from him, he would be watching you when you were training. He would pick up a VHS, click a button and show you the incident he had picked you up on, you had disagreed, and he would take you through the clip. You didn't have much of a leg to stand on after that, so I'd say, 'OK, Boss.' Fine, except training didn't start for a couple of hours, which meant hanging around with nothing to do. It would make you think twice about disagreeing with him again."

Parker is still considered to be part of the United 'family.' He was invited along with Denis Irwin and David May to join The Boss and the club's player-liaison officer Barry Morehouse on a trip to Cyprus to celebrate the Limassol Branch's 20th anniversary, accompanied by their partners. Paul takes up the scene where they are sitting outside a bar having a lovely time in the sunshine. "My wife turned around toward The Boss during the conversation and called Sir Alex 'Boss.' He looked at her and said, 'You don't call me Boss, but those three over there call me Boss, not you.' He said it with a big smile across his face, but somehow you knew he meant it. In private I might refer to him as Alex or Sir Alex, but every player past and present would call him Boss or Gaffer."

For Paul, there are three 'Gaffers' who stand out during his career. "I consider myself very, very fortunate to have played, in my opinion, for three of the greatest ever managers, in Jim Smith, Sir Alex Ferguson, and Sir

Bobby Robson. My one big regret is that I didn't play for Sir Bobby more often. Jim Smith was my first manager at QPR. It was a great learning curve for me to have worked under someone like Jim Smith. As for Sir Alex... he's at the top, and it was such a pleasure to have worked with him on a day-to-day basis."

Paul didn't say exactly what upset Sir Alex so much, but Neil 'Razor' Ruddock isn't shy in letting everyone know. The name of a famous Scottish TV detective was the insult that made Sir Alex's blood boil. Ruddock said, "I had a barney with Fergie – I kicked Mark Hughes on the halfway line at Old Trafford once, and Fergie came running – you know he used to come running onto the pitch? I said: 'F*** off, Taggart.' I just called him Taggart. I remember Bryan Robson coming up to me during the game saying, 'That's the funniest thing I've ever heard.' The changing rooms at Old Trafford, you used to turn right to go to the baths, and Fergie's office was halfway up there, so I used to s*** myself walking up through there in case he'd come out and get me."

FA Cup Opt Out

Garth Crooks was a young, aspiring BBC journalist when he witnessed Sir Alex striking out at the media. Crooks tells me, "Everybody is on tenterhooks when the press corps arrive at Manchester United, either at the training ground or at Old Trafford, if you know you have to deal with Alex Ferguson. You know in advance that if you ask a sharp question you will get a sharp answer. Personally I wouldn't expect anything else from him if I asked a sharp question. But I like him, I must say. I like him very much. I feel he is very fair and consistent ... at least, he has been with me, charming even, most of the time!

"There was one time when I arrived at Old Trafford to do an interview with him, totally unannounced, and you are always apprehensive about that. Manchester United had been drawn against Borussia Dortmund in the Champions League semi-finals and it was important to get the United manager to comment. But he didn't want to know. Instead of agreeing to my request for an interview on the *Foorball Focus* programme, he stuck by his prior arrangement to carry on with a local radio interview. Alex refused to do the interview with me, but he did allow me to interview the players, and I was grateful for that. As I said, tough but fair.

"Yet there was another occasion when I interrupted him with his family and friends having a meal at Old Trafford when there was a Simply Red concert on, and he not only agreed to my request for an interview – again not prearranged – he even apologised for keeping me waiting! I never thought I would get the interview, but I explained that there was no other time to do it and promised him it would only take a few minutes. The camera crew thought I had no chance as well. But the crew almost fell over when someone came out of the restaurant and said Fergie would be ready in about five minutes. We hung around. It was a nightmare because no one really thought he would come out and do the interview and would just walk away instead. To be honest, he would have been justified in doing so. But out he came, did the interview and was perfectly charming. Then he went back to his dinner. That is the side of Alex Ferguson that I should imagine few people experience... Admittedly, Manchester United had just won the league!"

One of Garth's early assignments was covering the World Club Championships in Rio. The task of being on the Copacabana Beach would fill a young BBC reporter with glee, but there was trepidation because this was one of the most controversial episodes in English football history. "The FA were told by FIFA that they had to instruct Manchester United to attend the World Club Championships as champions of England if England were going to stand any chance of winning the vote for the 2006 World Cup. It all became very much a political football with David Davies of the FA putting pressure on United to go to Rio, with United not wanting to go because it meant they would have to withdraw from the FA Cup and that was a hugely controversial decision.

"Some said at the time it would prove to be the death knell of the FA Cup and they were proved right, the FA Cup has never quite been the same since. With that as the backdrop, I was part of the BBC team sent out to Rio to cover the tournament. It was never going to be an easy assignment, and that's how it panned out. I had to visit the team's training camp on a regular basis with the task of interviewing Sir Alex virtually on a daily basis. On one occasion, I also had to work out with him the schedule of interviews on the match days, to go live before the game, then again at half-time, and finally immediately after the game. Despite his reputation with the media, I never felt anything but respect for him, and also felt he would reciprocate that respect as a fellow professional as he would have known I had played the game at the highest level, even for Manchester United.

"What I liked most about Sir Alex was that he was a football traditionalist, and in many ways I shared those sentiments about the game having been brought up under the management of Tony Waddington at Stoke and also George Eastham. I considered them, including Sir Alex, as respected gentlemen of the game, managers of the stature that fell into that category were Jock Stein, Alec Stock, Joe Mercer and Bertie Mee. They all graced the game and did things properly.

"Sir Alex might have been an intimidating character, but he was someone I was actually looking forward to spending time with, so it was a pleasure to be watching him and his team in training. Equally, I wanted to meet him well prepared, and I knew he was a great fan of Jock Stein and I wanted to do my research and have information up my sleeve so there was something to talk to him about while we were waiting to film, to discuss things he would be interested in such as the state of the game in Scotland and the great players who had emerged from Scottish football. So I had all these bits of information to talk to him about, to warm him up before our live interviews.

"I was sent by our head of sport Neil Sloane to the team hotel on the night before the first game with our producer Ian Finch to sort out the live interviews for the next day. I said to Finchie, 'Don't say one word to him, we might be walking on eggshells here, and if you say the wrong thing, he might go for your throat, chew you up and the relationship will be dead.' We get to the hotel and waited until Sir Alex had finished his evening meal, and while we awaited we set up the meeting with a couple of chairs by a table, and I told Finchie to make himself scarce, and wait outside.

"Sir Alex sat down and I explained to him all the timings for the interviews the following day through the course of the match, fifty minutes before kick-off, the interval, and after the game, and told him it was important for me and the BBC as it was a satellite feed we had put together which made it a big deal for the BBC. During our chat I asked him what Jock Stein was like. 'Jock, oh want a man, let me tell you about Jock Stein.' An hour later he was still talking about him! Not only that, he talked me through his tactical strategies, his great teams, and even got out the salt and pepper pots to illustrate it all. Of course, he had plenty of time on his hands, out in Brazil, and clearly enjoyed nothing better than to while away the hours talking football. For me it was fascinating to tap into Sir Alex's vast knowledge of the game.

"Throughout, he was just charming and gracious. He gave me an insight into a side of the man very rarely seen."

Pressure from the Government and the FA persuaded the club to ditch their defence of the FA Cup to participate in FIFA's new showpiece. The tournament didn't go well, drawing their first game with Mexico's Necaxa, Beckham was shown a red card for a thigh-high challenge, and Ferguson was sent off for complaining about the decision.

Out-classed by Vasco da Gama, with Romario and Edmundo dominant in a 3–1 win, United crashed out at the group stage, with their only win in three games at a largely empty Maracanã Stadium against Australian part-timers South Melbourne.

United recharged their batteries for their Premier League run-in. Accompanied by their own private security squad, they went for walks on the beach, chilled by the pool and did some training at altitude, ending up winning the title by eighteen points clear of the Gunners.

When the BBC crossed Sir Alex, it caught Garth off guard, "Sometime later, I was in Monaco working for the BBC for the Champions League draw and having built up a fine relationship with Sir Alex, was eagerly looking forward to interviewing him as it was sure to be a fascinating draw with United among the seeded clubs. Despite a good working relationship, I still knew he was not a man to take liberties with and when he emerged from the auditorium, I was very careful to be as polite as possible when I requested an interview.

"In front of a packed gathering of journalists and TV editors who were there working on their TV schedules of the games, he lurched into a screaming fit in my direction, 'I am not giving an interview for the BBC. I've told them I am not giving them nothing anymore, nothing, until they apologise to me.'

"I was shocked, taken aback, confused, and said, 'Sir Alex, what on earth is the matter?'

"To be fair to him, he could see I was shocked, that I didn't really know what he was going on about, but that didn't stop him, he continued the hairdryer treatment in front of a packed lobby. I was shattered by the experience. Of course, there was an issue going on in the background over the Panorama programme which had exposed his son's football agency business. I flipped at one of our producers Andrew Clement and told him I had been put in an embarrassing position. He said, 'So sorry, Garth, I didn't know anything about it, we are the sports department, not the news department.'"

Sir Alex did not departmentalise, as Garth observed, "I felt that I should have known he had taken this stand against the BBC, because he wasn't going to give a shit who from the BBC approached him, he had made up his mind to ostracise the BBC per se."

Garth witnessed a scarier confrontation in Rio with Sir Alex and journalist Martin Samuel. Garth recalled, "Sir Alex spotted Martin in the press conference and completely lost his temper, shouting at him about something in his paper concerning the club chairman Martin Edwards. But Martin wasn't having it. It was clearly not something Martin had written, and he hit back telling Sir Alex, 'I'm not having it.' Then Sir Alex left the podium and headed toward Martin, and Martin left his seat, and headed toward Sir Alex. They ended up virtually nose to nose, eyeball to eyeball, and I was sure if one of them had thrown a punch there would have been a ruck. But Sir Alex carried on walking and walked out of the press conference."

Despite the good and the bad, Garth's assessment of Fergie's career is glowing, "He must be one of the top all-time managers the UK has produced. He's up there with the best, like Paisley, Stein, Shankly and Sir Matt."

Stopping Players Going on
International Duty

Neil Webb played under Brian Clough. If you think Cloughie was a law unto himself, it was nothing compared to Sir Alex. Top of Webb's personal table of fall outs centred around his England call-up under manager Graham Taylor. England were playing in Czechoslovakia, and Taylor called up Webb, who was delighted and eager to participate as he had only played twice in two years, and the Euros were coming up. United were top, and Fergie wanted to keep his players fresh.

United took on Wimbledon prior to the midweek England game as Webb tells me, "I was substituted in the game at Old Trafford, and it wasn't the first time, I had been taken off around a dozen times already. But this time was different, because I was in the Players' Room as usual, when our physio Jim McGregor came in, and he told me, 'By the way, you are injured, and you are not going with England.'

"I told him, 'No, I'm not injured, what's this all about?'

Jim said, 'The Gaffer is not letting you go to report for England duty.' By the time I got home, I had a couple of calls waiting for me from journalists wanting to know about my England withdrawal through injury, and there was also a call from the England manager Graham Taylor to call him back urgently. I called Graham Taylor and told him that I wasn't injured and wanted to report for England duty. He told me, 'The club have told me that you can't come as you are injured, so you have a decision to make, and it's a tough one because if I don't see you, then you will be jeopardising your England career.' I sat back down and thought that I had been put into a ridiculous position. Do I let down England? Or do I let down my manager and my club? Clearly I didn't want to fall out with my manager as I have to work with him day in and day out. So I didn't report for England. Yet, when I turned up at the training ground on Monday morning, I trained. Of course I trained because I wasn't injured. The manager didn't care who would see me train, he wasn't in the least bit bothered, even though it proved I wasn't injured. And the manager picked me for the next game, and that again showed that I wasn't injured."

Webb received a message that Fergie wanted to see him in his office, "After a couple of days back training that week the manager called me to his office, and as I walked through the door a pen went flying past my head! He lurched straight into, 'What do you think you are doing?' I had no idea what he was talking about, but he quickly made it perfectly clear when he then said, 'You rang Graham Taylor…' I told him, 'I rang Graham Taylor because he rang me and left a message to call him, and yes I rang him and told him the truth – and you having me training all the time shows I wasn't injured.'

"That was it! If he was angry before, he now lost it, and in his thick Scottish accent I got it full barrels, and some of the words were pretty choice. He went into full rant mode and there was nothing I could say, if indeed he would have heard me had I spoken. That was my first and certainly my major fall out with him I thought Cloughie was a law unto himself, but this one was off the wall!"

Taylor picked him again. Webb tells me, "Graham Taylor picked me for a B team game in Moscow the following month, and I played in that game. I've no doubt that Graham Taylor had known what I had to go through, and I am sure I wasn't the only one to be put in such a tricky situation, as I am sure the same happened with Ryan Giggs with Wales and with Brian McClair with Scotland. The manager could pull a player out of an international squad for apparently no reason, although he probably had his reasons. But I couldn't see the reason why he did it to me, I couldn't understand it, it didn't make any sense to me at the time. What could I do about it? Nothing. So I got my head down and continued working hard in training."

Nicky Butt said Fergie used a rotation policy to keep England players back. "He never once said to me to fake an injury. He'd just say, 'You've got an England friendly coming up and you're not going.' And that was that. At one stage there was nine of us and he would pull one or two of us out and let the other six go."

Webb's final fall out was, "The one that broke the camel's back." He explains, "I had been a regular in the team toward the end of the season as we reached the Cup Winners' Cup Final. We travelled to Rotterdam for the final, and during breakfast, the manager called me over for a chat and he told me straight away, 'You're not starting.' I was shocked, and responded, 'Really, why?' He explained, 'I have opted to play Mike Phelan on the right-hand side to use his greater pace.' I was totally taken aback and failed to understand why he had taken that decision, and certainly even more baffled when he said he wanted to play Mike on the right instead of me, because I hadn't played on the right since I was seventeen! I was deeply disappointed, even more so as I didn't even get on, and yes, I sulked, I threw my toys out of the pram. When we arrived back, there was an open bus tour of the city, but I sat downstairs sulking. I had been deprived of a final that I might never get the chance to play in again.

"I asked for a meeting with the manager that summer and told him how desperate I was to play and how upset I was for being left out especially over the reasons given, and I told him, 'You took that chance away from me.' The manager said he was sympathetic and told me, 'Stick with it, stick with it…' Six months later he sold me back to Nottingham Forest. I was back in Nottingham, sitting in a hotel room and heard on the TV that Manchester United had bought Eric Cantona. I thought to myself, 'Now that will be interesting.' Eric wasn't that well known in English football at that time, despite his spell at Leeds United but I thought that was going to be a make or break situation for both manager and player, but as it turned out the signing was inspired and brought so much success to the club and to the manager, and I've no doubt that Fergie knew he had to treat Eric differently to get the best out of him, as no other player would have got away with what Eric did at Crystal Palace – they would have been out."

Glenn Hoddle rates Sir Alex the undisputed no. 1. Hoddle told me, "His record goes without saying, he is right up there. No one else has enjoyed that amount of success, over that length of time. For that reason Sir Alex commands respect from everybody in football. There have been some wonderfully outstanding managers like Bill Shankly, Sir Matt Busby, Bill Nicholson, and in modern times Jose Mourinho but Sir Alex built several teams, kept on re-inventing his sides and each time continued to win trophies. I don't think his record will ever be broken as I cannot see his record being surpassed by even the best of the modern-day managers."

Hoddle continues, "One issue in the game currently is the fact that managers are not given time, and for Sir Alex it wasn't winning major trophies in one season or over a short period of time, it was over a sustained period. He did it for years, then he looked like he would quit, didn't and built new teams and kept on winning major titles, all that took a mammoth effort on his part. It goes to show you what can happen when directors are prepared to give a manager time, something that doesn't happen now in modern football."

It always intrigues Hoddle 'What if' Sir Alex had moved from Aberdeen to Tottenham instead of United? Glenn explains, "At the time he was so successful at Aberdeen and was planning to come to English football, he was on the agenda of Tottenham, in fact, I know he was very close to coming to Tottenham. Yeah, he would have been ideal for Tottenham when you look at the way he gets his teams to play, very impressive. You have to admire what he did at Aberdeen, not a big club when you compare it to the giants of Rangers and Celtic, yet he took Aberdeen right up there with them and overtook them, even winning European trophies, so it wasn't just Manchester United who wanted him. Spurs were in there first, and they were right to want him. He has proved to be the most successful manager of his time, and he did it in the English league, the toughest one of all."

Hoddle understood the frustrations on both sides of the club vs country debate, as indeed would have Sir Alex who took charge of Scotland for a spell. Hoddle said, "As far as my time with England and what did or didn't happen then with Sir Alex is very much old hat. I met him a few times during my time in football over a glass of red wine after games."

Sir Alex's grievance was the way he perceived his treatment by the FA. He complained the FA treated United, 'like s***.' Paradoxically, Ferguson was proud his players would be called up. But he was still fuming over a touchline ban and a two-match suspension that ruled Rooney out of an FA Cup semi-final defeat to City. Asked about his England contingent, Ferguson said, "It is fantastic. The FA may realise who has produced more players for their country than any club. Maybe they will get some joy from it and realise how important we are to England instead of treating us like s***. I am pleased for the players. They are outstanding."

Sir Alex was in conflict with Hoddle during France '98, surprised that Darren Anderton started ahead of Beckham. What upset Hoddle were Ferguson's remarks about Hoddle's handling of Beckham. Ferguson felt Beckham shouldn't have been exposed to a media press conference over his exile from the team at the start of the campaign.

The red card against Argentina brought Ferguson and Hoddle head-to-head again. Fergie was determined to protect Becks against the backlash. Ferguson pointed an accusing finger at ITV interviewer Gary Newbon for laying the blame for defeat by Argentina on Beckham's sending-off. In an ITV interview, Ferguson said, "Glenn was asked an unfortunate question by our friend Gary Newbon on the final whistle. Gary asked Glenn about the sending-off – whether he thought it cost England the game. His natural reaction was to say yes. So Gary stirred a bit of a hornet's nest and everybody ran that the next day. I don't think Glenn meant what he actually said. The question was posed, and it was easy to say yes, but he corrected that the next day."

Hoddle recalled how he 'cheekily' tried to sign Beckham on loan when he was manager at Chelsea, Hoddle tells me,

"I do recall cheekily asking Sir Alex if I could have David Beckham on loan when David was just eighteen. I wanted a player like him, easy on the ball and would have put him straight into the first team, whereas Sir Alex had already loaned him out as he was gently easing him into his own first team. I got a flat 'No' from Sir Alex. He wasn't having it, and I fully understood, but if you don't ask, you don't get, so I thought it was worth a cheeky ask."

Sir Alex played a role in Scotland's World Cup build-up, running the rule over all the Scots' Group A opponents – holders Brazil, Norway and Morocco for manager Craig Brown, who said, "Alex's knowledge of the game is invaluable. I remember visiting him at United's training ground last year, and he showed me one of his most prized possessions. It was a photograph of United's 1992 youth team, nine of whom have gone on to become full internationals."

Confrontations

Kevin Keegan exploded during a live Sky Sports broadcast on 29 April 1996 – his unforgettable 'love it' meltdown. The perception is that Keegan and Sir Alex were daggers drawn then and remain so to this day. When I caught up with Kevin, he told me the real reasons behind it, "I first came up against him when I was playing with Southampton and we had what I considered at that time to be a fantastic team, with the likes of 'Bally', Mick Channon and Dave Watson, and we played in a tournament in Aberdeen. We played Fergie's Aberdeen in the Final, and we were well and truly beaten 5–1. All the way home on the coach we were thinking we were wrong about our side, that we must be crap to have been beaten so comprehensively by Aberdeen. We can't be much of a team when we had just been mullered by them, and we had put out our strongest team. But, of course, we knew very little to nothing about their manager back then, he was very young, as he had only just finished playing.

"When he came down to English football, people soon got to know who this guy was, but we had known about him a few years before, and then he went on to do something that probably will never happen again in Scottish football as he took Aberdeen to domestic and European glory with some incredibly gifted players like Gordon Strachan in midfield and Alex McLeish at the back, and quite a few of that team came down also to play in English football. As we all know Sir Alex had a tough time at first at Old Trafford but we also all know what he went on to achieve. Despite our rivalry on the field, after every game we always shook hands. Whether he beat us or we beat him, we always shook hands, there was always mutual respect.

"I've also met Sir Matt Busby and we were always big rivals when I played for Liverpool. When it comes to someone like Sir Alex, it is always hard to like someone when you are rivals. Sir Alex is different to me, that's for sure. I don't think he's the type who would want us to go out for dinner together! Sir Alex had a win at all costs mentality. He would do whatever it takes, and that is what you get used to, being a winner. I was a winner as a player but not quite so much as a manager. Do I respect him for what he has achieved? Yes, I do. Do I think he's the best we've had? Without doubt. Do I accept to go for a drink with him? Yes, if he's paying!

"However, I do recall one episode when he asked me to attend a function. He rang me up and said he had a mate who ran the Crow's Nest hotel up in Scotland, and he would be grateful if I would attend the function with him. He told me it wasn't far for me, just up the A1 near Edinburgh. Well, he stitched me up because when I arrived in Edinburgh, he told me it was near St. Andrews, fine as it was only ten miles as the crow flies, but it was almost sixty miles to get there by road. So off I went over the bridge, heading toward Dundee for twenty miles, turn right, and finally make it to St. Andrews. So, do we get on? Yes, we get on well."

Keegan embarked on his rant because Sir Alex claimed teams may not try as hard against Newcastle as they did against his side. Keegan was riled because Fergie suggested to Howard Wilkinson, that he would be happy to come to Leeds to give his players a pep talk before they faced Newcastle! Keegan believed Wilkinson was amenable to such a bizarre request. That is what really was behind the Keegan rant.

Sir Alex has few, if any, regrets, not even winding up Keegan! He said, "I have always thought that mind games and my supposed part in them were completely overrated. Sometimes I've said provocative things or tried to get my point of view across in advance of a game, because you try to get an edge wherever you can, but the Kevin Keegan incident was a complete accident. I was angry with the Leeds players because Howard Wilkinson was under pressure, and he's a mate of mine. I just made the point that Leeds should be playing as well as they played at Old Trafford all the time. I wasn't thinking of Newcastle at all." Sir Alex advised his successor to keep on top of referees, "That's been a part of it too, the pressure you try to put on referees, but I save mind games for opponents."

The flying pizza that struck Sir Alex in the tunnel of hate after a bitter clash with archrivals Arsenal is the stuff of football folklore. Cesc Fabregas threw a pizza after a heated game against the Gunners in October 2004. Ferguson was hit in the face by the flying pizza. Fergie discussed the Battle of the Buffet in his autobiography, "The next thing I knew I had pizza all over me. We put food into the away dressing room after every game. Pizza, chicken. Most clubs do it. Arsenal's food was the best. They say it was Cesc Fabregas who threw the pizza at me but to this day, I have no idea who the culprit was."

'Pizzagate' might be the cherry on the cake of the battle of the buffet but it was actually part of a feast of fiery red hot chilli encounters. Nigel Winterburn was blamed by Sir

Alex for the hors d'oeuvres in a series of tasty encounters. The left back brought plenty of bite, starting with a cup tie in 1988. Nigel told me, "Sir Alex blames me for starting it. It all started when Brian McClair missed a penalty in a cup game when George Graham was still our manager and I said to him, 'Thanks for missing the penalty.' Obviously he and the United players didn't take too kindly to my remark, in fact, it didn't go down too well at all, even though Brian McClair didn't say anything, his teammates had plenty to say about it.

"There have been quite a few issues between the two teams especially when both clubs were going strong, but Sir Alex blames me for lighting the fire, and why clashes always ended up exploding, and to be fair he might have a point, as what I did certainly didn't help relationships, so he's probably correct in what he says about me. Usually I don't mind lighting the fire, then disappearing out of sight and harm's way, but this time I was caught in the middle of it all! I was just pleased when Cesc Fabregas threw the pizza, because everyone then talked about that rather than what I got up to, which was a relief.

"Of course, looking back, I wish I hadn't done what I did, it was inappropriate, I think 'inappropriate' is a pretty polite word to use, but I shouldn't have had a go at someone for missing a penalty that's for sure. I am not proud of it, but things can happen in the heat of the moment, and our games with United were more often than not pretty heated. But nothing that happened on the field in those days can diminish what Sir Alex achieved, he built some unbelievable teams throughout the period he was in charge and we were incredible rivals. There were some big characters on both sides, none of whom would have wanted to back down, and didn't back down in those clashes, there were always those sorts of games. I have not met up with Sir Alex since I retired, so never had a chance to explain myself to him, not that he would be interested, I'm sure. You can probably imagine, though, that I am not on Sir Alex's Christmas card list!"

The antagonism dates back to Fergie's first encounter with the Gunners as United manager, a 2–0 defeat in 1987 when Norman Whiteside's wild challenges ended with retaliation from David Rocastle who was sent off. The rows continued after the final whistle in the Old Trafford tunnel. In 1990, it kicked off when McClair took exception to a Winterburn tackle that sparked one of the most notorious melees. The FA deducted Arsenal two points, United one. The Gunners overcame that punishment to claim the First Division title, winning their second title in three years.

Ray Parlour was one of the elite members of 'The Invincibles.' "Razor" tells me, "Sir Alex... the best there has ever been in the Premier League. Just look at his record, look at the number of trophies. I have never been in a dressing room with Sir Alex as my manager, but I can imagine what it would have been like. Sir Alex knew what he wanted, the players knew what he wanted, and his players knew they had to do exactly what he said, and they knew the consequences if they didn't. Whatever the players might have thought about his strict regime the manager was well respected for delivering the results. Those results turned into numerous trophies, his record is simply amazing. He had his ups and downs early on, but once he got it the way he wanted, there was no stopping him and his teams, although at Arsenal at the time we did our best to spoil it for him.

"We always said that our hardest game of the season was the North London derby because it meant so much to our fans, but our biggest games of the season were against Manchester United, and we always felt that if we could take four points from Manchester United we could go all the way and win the title. Our encounters with United were not only physical, they turned into battles as much as good football. There was an awful lot of good football but when we finished and were back in our dressing room I had never seen so many ice packs being applied to so many bumps and bruises, but I knew there would be just as many in their dressing room getting the same treatment if not more. Every time we came together it was a high intensity game, and you sense the intensity in the stadiums as soon as you walk out, the crowd were always creating an incredible atmosphere, and it gave us enormous pleasure actually winning the league at Old Trafford, and we knew what Sir Alex had told his players, 'Don't let those Cockney ***** beat us.' But we did beat them and won the league.

"We had some famous games with United in those years, and most people will remember an FA Cup semi-final and Ryan Giggs' wonder goal racing from the halfway line. There was a game I still recall when Patrick Vieira was sent off, there were penalties, and last minute winners, all sorts went on, but of course Martin Keown and I had left by the time of the 'Pizzagate' incident, but Martin was the man who started all the trouble when he goaded Van Nistelrooy when he missed a penalty, but I ended up getting a ten grand fine from the FA when there was a bit of a scuffle toward the end. There were four of us fined, Martin got the biggest fine, twenty grand, and I was fined along with Ashley Cole and Lauren."

Razor and Sir Alex share a love and interest in horses and racing, "I met Sir Alex a few times on various racetracks, I used to own a couple of horses and Sir Alex always owned horses. Whenever I met up with him, nothing was ever mentioned about our rivalry, we talked about the horses and I found him a really good guy."

Sam Hammam explained in an exclusive interview for my previous book on Ferguson, "What makes Alex Ferguson so special, the most distinguished manager of his generation, is that not only has he been such a success at Manchester United – he would have also been successful had he been manager of Wimbledon or Doncaster or even Halifax. I have come to know him over the years. Whenever Manchester United come to London to play us, they stay at their hotel overnight and Alex arrives early to have a chat. We sit and talk for ages and I have come to recognise that he does not live in an ivory tower like some manager who represents one of the elite. Alex is not interested in after dinner speaking, polishing his TV personality or opening shops. He is, though, one of the hardest workers in the game. He also knows everyone in his youth team, he's met their parents and has done his homework. That is his great strength. He has concentrated on the youth and reserve teams and hasn't had to just throw money at buying players. He takes an interest in every aspect of the club and knows about the finances. He knows the nitty-gritty of running a football club rather than being in cloud cuckoo land.

"Most managers would say, 'Give me £10 million to buy the best player available.' But running clubs at Wimbledon or Doncaster encompasses far more awareness than that. He is a detailer and a worker with knowledge deeply rooted about the workings of a football club rather than being a big-time Charlie. Anyone who had achieved as much success as Alex might be in danger of losing a few screws. Instead he has shown himself to be a man of steel; no screws lost."

Hammam saw the Fergie red mist in one of the most infamous clashes in football – the so-called 'Tunnel of Hate' when Viv Anderson and John Fashanu had some pre-half-time 'discussions' en-route to the Plough Lane dressing rooms. Hammam witnessed the violence. He recalled, "John Fashanu and Viv Anderson fought in the tunnel. Viv ended up needing treatment in the Manchester United dressing room, while John Fashanu was sitting in our dressing room. Alex Ferguson came tearing down the tunnel and he wanted to enter our dressing room to beat up John Fashanu. All the king's horses and all the king's men weren't going to stop him. That is, apart from Don Howe. Don was standing there in the middle of the narrow entrance with both arms spread out to reach either wall. Don was emphatic, 'No, Alex, no, you're not going in there.'

"There was no doubt, as far as I was concerned, that Alex was not simply going in there to give Fash a piece of his mind. He was ready to fight him. Alex is tough as nails, and very single-minded. He was furious. He was out to protect his own and I don't blame him for that. I am not going to reveal precisely what Alex was saying but, judging by his state of mind, he was ready to fight the whole damn troop, let alone Big Fash. We have talked about it since. He can laugh about it now."

Telling Sir Alex to 'f*** off' led to the worst 'hairdryer' treatment he received. Gary Neville has frequently described the Champions League visit to Lille in 2007 that led to two away games in the stands as punishment. He calls it, 'the most serious confrontation' he endured. He said, "I once told him to FO. Not a good call. We scored from a quick free-kick while Lille were assembling their wall. After protesting to the ref, they started walking off. 'Come on, get on with the f****** game,' I said to their captain, following him towards the side of the pitch. The next thing I knew the manager was charging down the touchline, shouting at me, 'What are you doing? Get back on!' As far as I was concerned, I'd been doing the sensible thing, trying to get everyone to get on with a game we were now leading. So I snapped back 'F*** off' and walked away. Now, I've said 'f*** off' a million times to a lot of different people but never to the manager before. I knew I wasn't going to get away with it. Afterwards I got a call to go and see The Boss in his office. He was apoplectic. He blitzed me. We were playing at Fulham at the weekend, and he took me all the way down to London and didn't even put me on the bench. Three days later he took me down to Reading and left me in the stands again. The trip was a total waste of time, but The Boss had asserted his authority. I wouldn't be swearing at him again."

Fergie drew the line with Roy Keane after an explosive appearance on MUTV following a 4–1 defeat to Middlesbrough when Keano criticised his teammates for not being good enough. The rant earned a £5,000 fine. A training-ground bust-up involved Keane, assistant Carlos Queiroz, Edwin van der Sar and Fergie. Queiroz accused Keane of showing a lack of loyalty to his teammates. Ferguson stepped in, saying, "That's enough. I've had enough of all this stuff." Keane responded, "You as well, gaffer. We need f****** more from you. We need a bit more, gaffer. We're slipping behind other teams." When Van der Sar suggested Keane could have used a 'different tone' the reply, "Edwin, why don't you shut the f*** up? You've been at this club for two minutes and you've done more interviews than I've done in my twelve years. It was MUTV – I had to do it." Fergie observed, "I think the dressing room relaxed when Roy left. Relief swept the room. They no longer had to listen to the barrage that some of them had grown to expect."

The King of Old Trafford was spared a scolding after jumping into the crowd and kung-fu kicking a Crystal

Palace fan during a 1–1 draw at Selhurst Park in 1995. Fergie was more enraged at dropped points, with former winger Lee Sharpe recounting, "Cups of tea and plates of sandwiches. They were sent f****** flying everywhere." On Cantona's red card – which he later received a nine-month ban for – Ferguson said after chastising the rest of the team, "And Eric... [in a softer tone] you can't go round doing things like that, son..."

Keith Gillespie tells me, "I left United on 10th January for Newcastle and the following week it all kicked off with Eric at Palace, and Lee Sharpe loves telling the story of what happened in the dressing room. He tells a great story. The manager was in a foul mood, all the players could see it, the team had drawn 1–1 and Sir Alex went around the dressing room having a go at all the players: 'You never caught a cross, Peter Schmeichel, David May, you never picked up your guy and he scored the goal'... he even had a go at Ryan Giggs, 'Ryan Giggs, you never got one cross in'... 'Paul Ince, how many tackles did you make, not one' and 'Eric Cantona, you can't do that sort of thing!'

"I was not surprised one bit to hear it, because Sir Alex knew how to handle his players, and knew that Cantona was a special case, and needed to be handled in a different way. Eric was temperamental, and you knew if the manager gave him stick, he could easily just get up and walk out, for good."

Cantona will always be indebted to Ferguson for believing in him. He says, "The manager signed me in the first place knowing the risk he might have been taking if he had believed all the tales he had heard about me. He enjoyed himself in a magnificent career as a player and manager. Although when he advised me about the rights and wrongs of retaliation he let slip that he had been sent off more times than I had."

Paul Parker adds, "Yes, there are so many examples of 'The Boss' giving players the hairdryer treatment, and I was on the receiving end myself, but Eric. No. Not Eric. He never did. The Boss loved him, in the sense, that he could almost do whatever he wanted, and it is fair to say that The Boss was a little bit more lenient with him than he would be with the rest of us. But there was a good reason, method behind this seeming madness. The Boss knew that Eric needed a special kind of man management. The Boss knew that this was a player of rare talent, but also there must have been reasons why he couldn't settle at all the clubs he had been with and didn't think the right approach was to fight fire with fire, maybe the way Eric had been treated elsewhere. The Boss thought that rather fight fire with fire, he would throw a bucket of water on it! He would treat Eric with a fire blanket."

Parker's favourite Cantona story is the one he selects because it is not only hilarious but perfectly illustrates the way The Boss, made him an exception. "The players used to attend events at the Town Hall virtually every year, either Stratford Town Hall or Old Trafford Town Hall, as a celebration of winning a major trophy, so it was virtually every summer after we had won something. We would all sit down with all the local councillors and dignitaries, in the sort of occasion that The Boss insisted that we were turned out fully kitted out in club blazer with the club badge, club tie with the club badge, and the perfect grey club trousers and black shoes, everyone looking immaculate just as The Boss would expect, and no exceptions. Well, not Eric. He was a law unto himself, so in he walked... he had the club blazer with the club badge alright, but he had the lapels trimmed down looking vastly different to the 'table tennis' lapels of the 90s. He also had a trimmed black tie, yes it had the club badge, but it was something Paul Weller would have worn back then. Trousers, yes regulation grey, but tapered, again in the style of Paul Weller. As for the shiny black shoes we were all wearing, buffed up and polished to within an inch of their lives. No, in he strode in red Nike trainers. We all looked at each other, and looked at The Boss, we all waited for a reaction, we had no clue what would happen, but we all expected The Boss to explode. We were shocked when there wasn't the reaction we expected. The Boss smiled! And he said to Eric, 'Eric, only you could dress like that and look that good' That summed up the way The Boss managed Eric Cantona, demonstrated how much he wanted Eric to feel wanted, loved, and respected, not brow beaten.

"To be fair, The Boss was right, Eric was one of those people who looked incredible, whatever he was wearing. Some people could have walked into that room wearing a £1,000 suit and Eric could have got his gear from Oxfam for fifty quid, but he would have looked the part."

Sir Alex almost signed Peter Beardsley ahead of Cantona. Beardsley told me, "I really had no idea that Fergie wanted to sign me until I read it in his book. I didn't even know he had spoken to Newcastle, I was totally unaware. He certainly didn't speak with me, no tapping up! There weren't mobile phones in those days. I had been at United when Big Ron was manager, but I have to confess I wasn't up to it, not good enough and moved on to Vancouver. It was fascinating to read that Fergie came for me around the time when I moved to Liverpool. It would have been interesting if I had the choice between Liverpool and United. To be fair, I would have chosen Liverpool, and that is not in any way being critical of Sir Alex, because he made them unbelievable, but I would have always chosen Liverpool because of Kenny Dalglish. He was my hero as a kid, I loved him, and when he signed me he gave me the no. 7 shirt at Liverpool at a time when the no. 7 shirt meant something really special, it was the number worn by Kenny and by Kevin Keegan. It was always special to wear the numbers one to eleven, but now you can wear twenty-seven or thirty-two, and it has no meaning, but the no. 7 shirt meant something really special to me because of who had worn it before at Anfield, even though, of course, I was nowhere near as good as those two, but happy if ever anyone considered me being third best behind real superstars of the game. I have never had the chance to talk to Sir Alex about it, although I have seen him a few times, but not long enough to have discussed it. He was always very complimentary, even when Newcastle beat his team 5–0, although he wasn't happy, he was a gentleman about it, coming onto the pitch and holding his hands up."

Sir Alex's development of young talent has been spectacular. David Beckham is on record as saying, "The first time I really got into the squad the manager wasn't using me a lot. I was on the bench and sometimes I wasn't even getting changed. That kept me hungry. I always wanted to be there. And once I got a taste for it, I felt sort of embarrassed if I wasn't there." When Becks first thought he had made it, he was loaned out to Preston. He revealed in *Arena* magazine, "The Boss certainly gives you confidence – but he doesn't give you too much of it. He can bring you into the first team for training for two days on the trot. And then for two weeks you won't be training with the first team again. That was how it went. But, as I say, that's what kept me hungry."

Posh and Becks were box office, but for Sir Alex it was an unwanted distraction. Teammates had to intervene following the infamous flashpoint after United were defeated by Arsenal in the 2003 FA Cup fifth round at Old Trafford. In the dressing room a furious Fergie singled out Beckham, who swore back. Spotting a pile of boots, Ferguson kicked one which struck Beckham above his left eye. Players stepped in. "The next day the story was in the press," Ferguson recalled. "In public an Alice band highlighted the damage inflicted by the boot. It was in those days that I told the board David had to go." Beckham was sold to Real for £25m. "If I tried it 100 or a million times it couldn't happen again," Fergie reflected.

Tom Watt, best known for his role in *EastEnders*, tells me, "As the ghost writer to David Beckham's book, I don't think I would necessarily figure on Sir Alex's Christmas card list, although he probably doesn't even know me as his former player's ghost writer. My impression was then, when David's book was published, that the United manager was not greatly impressed. It was to be the last book to emerge from Old Trafford by one of their current players that didn't have full editorial approval and total control by the club – and I think that tells its own story. But having written David's book for him, I know how much David respects Fergie. They had their ups and down, of course, but David's admiration for his manager at the time remains undiminished, limitless. In fact I can safely say that David still regards Fergie as the biggest single person to have impacted on his footballing career. They had their clashes during their later years together at Manchester United, but David still thinks the world of the bloke."

Watt experienced an unusual confrontation with Sir Alex, which actually turned out far better than he expected, "The one time I remember most was the time I was presenting a kids' sports show for Channel Four in the 1990s, where the kids were presenters and the kids also did the interviews. We were hoping to do a bit of filming at The Cliff, the old Manchester United training ground where these kids could interview the kids in the club's Academy.

I don't know how it all happened, but it all started with a phone call to the club to ask who the best person would be to speak with to try to make it happen. I was given a number and told that I should ring it to see if we could do the filming at the club's fabled academy. I rang the number, and to my surprise it took me straight through to The Cliff… it was Alex Ferguson's private number in his office there!

"Sir Alex picked up the phone and when I introduced myself and tried to explain why I was calling, I could hear this gravelly Scottish voice swearing and bellowing, 'How did you get this number?' He was steaming, furious. I tried to tell him it's about the kids, but I wasn't sure how this was going to end up, either he would continue to go absolutely crazy, or he would just hang up. He did neither. Once I had got over the point that it was the kids in a sports show for kids wanting to connect with their peers at the academy, he couldn't have been nicer, couldn't have been more cooperative. His mood completely changed. He got it and wanted to help make it happen. 'Just say you have spoken to me and I'm happy with it.'

"He was terrifying to start with, then charming and helpful at the end. The conversation lasted around ten to fifteen minutes, when I made that call from our production offices, and I'll never forget it. It was post *EastEnders*, but I doubt whether he ever watched it, so he wouldn't know who I was, I'm sure he had much better things to do on a Tuesday and Thursday night."

Wayne Rooney sought Sir Alex's advice on management when about to takes his first steps with Derby. Yet they had numerous fall-outs. Rooney says, "It's documented we had disagreements, but disagreements are good in football. The best way to motivate me? Confrontation. I've always been at my best when I've been a bit angrier. Fergie knew exactly what I needed. I'd say ninety per cent of the games I played under him we were arguing at half-time. I used to think, 'I'm playing well, he'll have a go at someone else today.' And it would be me again. Portsmouth was the worst one. I went back out and scored a hat-trick. I remember sitting on the coach thinking, 'I've gone too far there' but the good thing about him, he'd go to the toilet in the coach or to get a coffee and walk past you on the way back and just, like, slap you on the back of the head. That was his way of saying, 'The argument is gone.' He never carried grudges.

"It spurs some of the lads on, but it crushes others. I've seen the manager shout and scream at people and when they've gone back on the pitch their heads have dropped. They've lost it. I don't think you will get better than how he managed his players and the trust he gave them to manage the dressing room themselves. That's management. It's the best I've ever seen. It wasn't complicated. The big thing was he had trust in people. He trusted his coaches to put sessions on, he trusted his players. People always ask how were his team talks? A lot of his team talks were just, 'You eleven are better than them. Go win the game.'

"I was in a dressing room with Gary Neville and Roy Keane. I was nineteen having rows with Gary, even with Alex Ferguson. That's how it should be. Sir Alex was really clever like that. He knew who he could have a go at, who it was best to leave alone. He always knew it brought the best out of me. It wouldn't work with Nani."

Rooney recalled one of Sir Alex's most explosive moments after United lost 1–0 at Celtic in a Champions League group game in 2006. Louis Saha missed a last-minute penalty as United lost to Gordon Strachan's side. Ferguson and Strachan had 'previous.' The United boss gave Saha both barrels. "It's the worst 'hairdryer' I've seen," said Rooney. "He was in Louis' face shouting and screaming. But Louis wasn't the only one getting an earful. The manager knew I'd been negotiating a new deal with the club and he saved some for me... 'Players wanting more money from the club and new deals – you don't deserve anything after that performance!'"

Fergie laid into his players before they went out to lift the Premier League trophy in 2007. United won the title with two games to spare, But they lost at home to West Ham on the final day. In his autobiography *My Decade*, Rooney recollected, "Most sides would be celebrating in the dressing room, getting ready for the champagne and the photos. Not us. We're staring at the floor like schoolkids, the manager giving us the 'hairdryer'. After the rollicking it takes a while before everyone cheers up enough to put their Premier League-winning smiles back on. There's nothing worse than getting the 'hairdryer' from Sir Alex. When it happened to me, the manager stood in the middle of the room and lost it at me. He got right up in my face and shouts. It felt like I'd put my head in front of a BaByliss Turbo Power 2200. It's horrible when it happens. I don't like getting shouted at by anyone. It was hard for me to take, so sometimes I shouted back. I told him he's wrong and I'm right."

Ferguson confessed, "I admit I gave Wayne a few rollickings. He would rage in the dressing room when I picked him out for criticism. His eyes would burn as if he wanted to knock my lights out. The next day he would be apologetic. When the anger subsided he knew I was right – because I was always right, as I used to tease him."

Ruud van Nistelrooy and Thierry Henry competed for the golden boot in the 2001–02 season. United were at home to Charlton on the final day, with Van Nistelrooy in with a chance of being top scorer in his first year in the Premier League. United finished third with Arsenal champions. "I was challenging but the gaffer left me out in the last game of the season," Ruud explained. "He said, 'You're not challenging for the golden boot. We didn't win the league, son. You're out.' He left me in the stands, not even on the bench! There wasn't even a hope for coming on." Henry's twenty-four for the season edged van Nistelrooy by one. Sir Alex's psychology worked as the following season, van Nistelrooy was top with twenty-five.

Left out of the squad for the final game of the season, van Nistelrooy reacted by driving away from Old Trafford three hours before kick-off. Four years later van Nistelrooy apologised. Recalling an unexpected text, Ferguson said, "My phone beeped with a text message. 'I don't know whether you remember me' it started 'but I need to call you.' I had no idea what it might be. But I texted back 'OK'. So he rang. First, the small talk. Had some injuries, fit now, not getting a game, blah blah. Then he came out with it. 'I want to apologise for my behaviour in my last year at United.' Ruud offered no explanation. Perhaps I should have taken that chance to say, 'Why did it go that way?'"

United crashed to a 3–1 defeat at City in November 2002, Fergie was incensed to see his striker return to the dressing room without his shirt but with a sky-blue jersey. Fergie screamed, "You do not give away one of those shirts. They're my shirts. They're this club's shirts, they're not your shirts. You're just wearing them temporarily. That's not your possession to give away." Gary Neville remarked, "He stopped us swapping shirts in domestic games. I think he said after that game, 'I should let the fans in here. I should let the fans come in here and speak to you.'"

Sir Alex also stopped his players swapping shirts with their Leeds counterparts after an FA Cup shock. Leeds, who were in League One at the time, stunned United at Old Trafford in the third round in 2010. Jermaine Beckford scored the only goal as Leeds became the first lower league side to ever knock Fergie's United out of the FA Cup. He was furious with Rooney, Berbatov and Gary Neville. Beckford said, "After the game, a couple of the boys had family who were Manchester United fans. They tried to get a couple of shirts from their players and Alex Ferguson said, 'Absolutely not, under no circumstances are you giving any of them your shirts.'"

Thirteenth of April 1996. Sir Alex's most bizarre melt down at half time – blaming his team's kit colour. A run of eleven wins in twelve eroded a commanding twelve-point lead from Keegan's Newcastle, but Sir Alex's team were having a nightmare at The Dell, 3–0 down to a team in the middle of a relegation dogfight. Lee Sharpe remembered, "The manager just stormed in and said, 'Get that kit off, you're getting changed.' Those were the first words he said at half-time." United changed into blue and white and 'won' the second forty-five minutes 1–0, but still lost 3–1 with Giggs scoring a minute from time. United won every remaining fixture to take the title.

Sir Alex's 'hairdryer' inspired as well as intimidated. The epic 5–3 victory over Tottenham at The Lane in September 2001 stands out. Trailing 3–0 at half-time, the players suffered their manager's 'hairdryer' and United staged an extraordinary comeback. Juan Sebastian Veron revealed that a dressing-down from Fergie inspired the fightback, "I've never been involved in anything like it. El Mister, Ferguson, was not happy at half-time. He said we had no respect for the people. We scored five in the second half."

Veron was one of the world's greatest midfield players when he arrived at Old Trafford for a record fee, but the media's persistence over his fluctuating form provoked one of the manager's trademark eruptions. United were 'welcoming' Arsenal to Old Trafford when they were set to land the title. Fergie did not relish the questions from journalists in the build-up. As Wenger's team needed a point to confirm their second Premiership and FA Cup double in four years, Fergie was in a foul mood with his team on the brink of finishing empty-handed for only the third time in thirteen years. Fergie unleashed his frustrations with a rant against his critics before ordering the journalists to "Get out" of the training ground. Ferguson told reporters, "He's a f****** great player… youse are all f****** idiots."

At the end of a 6–1 home drubbing to City in October 2011, a couple of weeks before Sir Alex's 25th anniversary at Old Trafford, the players knew what awaited them. He was furious at the club's biggest derby defeat since January 1926. With ten men following Jonny Evans' red card early in the second half, United conceded three late goals. City went on to win their first Premier League title. Fergie said, "It's the worst result in my history, ever. Even as a player I don't think I ever lost 6–1. I can't believe the score-line." He was 'shattered' and 'embarrassed.'

Gary Pallister formed half of arguably United's greatest central defensive with Steve Bruce, 'Dolly and Daisy' sharing a trophy-laden seven seasons together. Pallister's brace of headers against Liverpool at Anfield virtually clinched the 1997 title. Yet a raging Sir Alex 'battered' him for accidentally leaking his new dead ball training ground secrets. During the 1996–97 season, Sir Alex started to take their set-piece tactics more seriously after some advice from the army! In the week ahead of a top-of-the-table clash with their bitter rivals, Fergie kept his players late after training to work on corners and free-kicks, concentrating on Beckham's right foot deliveries. United reaped the rewards, with Pallister scoring twice – the only time he managed the feat – in a 3–1 win at Anfield. In the dressing rooms, Pallister took a blow to the head for revealing United's secret ahead of a huge Champions League clash with Borussia Dortmund. Pallister revealed, "We very rarely did set pieces. The manager had a letter from an ex-army major, talking about decoys, saying we should incorporate them into our set pieces. We went to Liverpool, I think we were first and second, and we scored two from set pieces and it was probably the game that decided the title that season. We were about to play Borussia Dortmund in the semi-finals of the Champions League. So I'm in the dressing room celebrating, the gaffer's gone out to do an interview, where unbeknown to me they ask him about the set pieces. He said it was just something off the cuff, so I'm oblivious to all this. The next thing I get the knock to go out and have a chat with the cameras and talk about the game. I'm thinking too right I will, so I'm going out there full of beans and it's, 'Yeah, Pally, talk us through the goals.' So I've said, 'It's something we've been working on all week.' I've done that and I've come back in the dressing room and the manager's battered me across the back of the head, going apoplectic with rage. He was like, 'What are you doing telling Borussia Dortmund we've been working on set pieces all week?' You can't do right for doing wrong... I scored two goals at Anfield to help us win the league, and still got a rollicking." United lost 1–0 to Dortmund in Germany, crashing out of the Champions League in the semi-final stage 2–0 on aggregate.

Pally tells me how highly he rates Sir Alex, "Quite remarkable, I'd suggest – that's the only way to describe him. To do what he did is remarkable, in terms of building up his reputation with a phenomenal job at Aberdeen, disrupting the Old Firm, up there, something that was a little bit special to say the least, as I can't recall that ever happening before or since, and that catapulted him toward United. What he then did at United was quite remarkable as well, if not more so, and that puts him among the pantheon of great managers. Is he THE greatest... wow, that is hard to answer. It's so hard to judge between different eras, and managers who have won, say, a World Cup, but Fergie won the Champions League twice, but more importantly his longevity, to be at a club the size of Manchester United for such a long time, I don't think that will happen again. If you are assessing who is the best, then Sir Alex is certainly in the mix, right up there at the top of it."

Pally found Sir Alex unique, "Sir Alex would join the players at the back of the bus, more than once, in fact quite often. He loved joining in the card schools. We loved the game of 'Hearts' where you would gang up on the leader and pass on cards, but if you passed on cards that Fergie didn't like he would often explode and throw his cards down the aisle of the bus. It wasn't that he was desperate to win, he just hated losing, and became very frustrated if he wasn't dealt the cards he wanted. I am sure he would now be embarrassed by that sort of thing, and probably claim it never happened. But he was similar to myself, he got bored, he didn't just want to sit in front of the telly or listen to music, he liked to be involved in everything.

"Usually it would be me, Robbo, Steve Bruce and the Gaffer playing cards at the back of the bus, but sometimes it might be Brian McClair or our physio Jim McGregor. Those games were great fun, but it also gave us an insight into what The Gaffer was really like. We certainly knew if he was pissed off, because those cards would go flying. The rest of us tried hard not to snigger when he lost his temper, because we didn't mind, we all thought it was hilarious."

In April 1988, Liverpool won the title for the 10th time in sixteen years. Ferguson was struggling at United, and the teams drew 3–3 but Ferguson, furious at the dismissal of defender Colin Gibson, was in the tunnel complaining about referee intimidation at Anfield. Dalglish, carrying his six-week-old daughter, interrupted the radio interview and suggested that the journalist talk to the babe-in-arms rather than Ferguson. "My daughter talks more sense than you do," he said to Ferguson. Fergie was livid. "I now understand why clubs come away from here biting their tongues and choking on their vomit, knowing that they have been done by referees."

Ferguson, though, was quick to offer sympathy after Hillsborough, one of the first on the phone to Dalglish. When Ferguson was under severe pressure in his early United days, it was Dalglish who stood up at a Football Writers' Association dinner defending Fergie's abilities. Ferguson's physiotherapist, Jim McGregor, took Dalglish aside a few weeks later and said, "By the way, the gaffer needed that."

Another pair of Scots have history. Two men born just eleven miles apart in Glasgow. George Graham, when he was the Arsenal boss, once brawled with Ferguson in the tunnel at Old Trafford. Graham said, "I remember when Alex first came down to take over at United. I had never met him and I was dying to find out all about this manager who had done so well in Scotland. Arsenal got beaten. We ended up fighting in the tunnel, and slagging each other off. But I don't know why Scots managers are so successful. Maybe it's because of our passion for the game – part of the Scottish character."

Graham was instrumental in gaining Sir Alex his first big pay rise at Old Trafford. Sir Alex finally landed silverware and went to chairman Martin Edwards in search of a new deal. George was the highest paid manager in the First Division and tells me, "Alex phoned me out of the blue.

He wanted to know what I was earning. I told him, 'I can't tell you exactly.' I gave him what I thought was a good answer, 'I will tell you, though, that I am earning between £X and £X.' Before I knew what was happening, Alex had gone to his chairman Martin Edwards and told him, 'George is earning £X, so should I.' I found out because Martin Edwards had gone to someone at Arsenal and asked if it was true that George is earning that much. He was told, 'Bloody hell, George is earning much more than that!'" The inference is that Fergie came to a figure and it was actually less than what Graham was earning at Highbury. George added, "Alex wanted an exact figure, but I never told him the figure, I told him to 'figure it out for yourself'."

The Agents He Loved... and Hated

Pini Zahavi is a football agent who has been involved in some of the biggest high-profile transfers. Few football agents were closer to Sir Alex. I caught up with the globe-trotting super-agent at his Tel Aviv offices. Prior to this interview, he insisted, "Is this for Sir Alex or against him? What will your book be about?" My response was positive, as I explained the ethos of the book was a tribute.

Pini told me, "Yes, he was the best, the greatest, there will never be someone like him, never be a second Sir Alex Ferguson in world football. The game has changed, it is different now. He managed everything, he was manager, coach, and CEO. What he achieved was simply incredible. I was with Sir Alex a lot, I admired him, got to know him. Of course, sometimes he was not an easy man, but I have met a lot of managers in my time and in my life, but Sir Alex is, no doubt, very special, unique. Look, no one is 100 per cent perfect, but in football Sir Alex was an amazing guy, and in the history of the game, he will have an important place for ever."

Zahavi was instrumental in taking Rio Ferdinand from West Ham to Leeds for £18m and then on to United for £30m in 2002. "For me, the three best signings I had been involved with was to bring Sir Alex Ronaldo, Rio, and Tevez. They were certainly the three best signings from my side that I did with him and Manchester United." Pini first mooted moves for Ronaldo and Rio when they were young boys. He tells me; "Yes, it was not easy at the beginning with Ronaldo, because he was so young. He was just a boy. But I managed to convince Sir Alex to take him. He was the first one I brought to Sir Alex, then Rio. When Rio was at West Ham, I recommended to Sir Alex to take him, but again he was so very young, and Sir Alex didn't think he was ready. Rio went to Leeds, and there he convinced Sir Alex that he was the right player for Manchester United and he took him then. But, yes, it is true that he could have taken him earlier, but once he was playing so well at Leeds, it didn't take Sir Alex long to make up his mind to take him.

"Tevez! It took Sir Alex two minutes to agree to take Tevez. When I spoke with Sir Alex he told me, 'Yes, bring him.' All three were top, top players for Sir Alex." Pini remains a close friend and confidante and became involved in a number of other high-profile deals. He helped to sell Jaap Stam to Lazio and played a part in Veron's transfer to United.

José Kléberson Pereira was born in the southern state of Paraná, rising through the youth ranks to become a first-team regular, claiming two Paraná State League titles and, more impressively, the Brazilian Série A in 2001. He burst onto the international scene during a successful 2002 World Cup campaign after impressing for Athletico Paranaense. He came to the attention of Barry Silkman, who recommended him to David Sullivan, at that time chairman of Birmingham City. Silkman tells me, "I thought he was alright, skilful, but perhaps lacking the physical attributes for English football, but worth a try if he was cheap. In Brazil I was put in touch with a guy called

Alex Lourez, and I met him at Heathrow Airport holding up a board with his name as I assumed he wouldn't speak a word of English, or very little. Someone comes up to me and says, 'Are you Silk?' Everyone called me 'Silk' or 'Silky' and they still do. 'Yes I am,' I told him, and he said I looked a bit different than he expected. But as he spoke, I'm hearing a Cockney accent and perfect English. He said he was born just outside of Rio, but I asked him if he was who he said he was, and he got out his passport to prove it. He explained that he had lived in Hackney from the age of about seven and had gone to study at Hackney college. He was in his thirties and when I said I'd take him to a hotel, he said he was fine as he was staying with some friends in Shoreditch.

"The next day I took him to meet David Sullivan in Birmingham and suggested that he could fix up a loan deal for the players with an option to buy at three million dollars, around £2m at that time. Alex pointed out that he wasn't sure he could cope with English football so it was decided to give him a try on a loan agreement and I would be entrusted to do all the ins and outs with Alex acting in Brazil, and we hung around while all the forms and agreements were drawn up. A week goes by and we heard nothing, only to then discover that Alex Ferguson had had him watched and was interested in taking him to United. Alex back in Brazil couldn't believe it, especially as United had offered close to £8m. I told him, 'He can't play for United, he's not right for them, at best he should come to Birmingham.' He ended up in Manchester where I went up there to meet him, his dad, and his young wife, and made my point that he would be better off in Birmingham but left them all to it and returned to London.

"Alex [Lourez] later told me he had signed for United, and that Alex Ferguson was watching him train. The bloke who scouts for the club came over to the manager and asked whether he had signed Kleberson? Alex told him that he had signed him, 'So, where is he?' he was asked. When Alex pointed him out, the scout said, 'That's not him!'

"This is what must have happened. His club Athletico Paranaense play in black and white striped shirts, and Kleberson was wearing the no. 7, but he was watching a player who had 17 on his shirt, but the one was obscured by the stripes! They had got the wrong player, and I don't think I have heard of something like that in all my years."

Kleberson was at United for two years before moving to Besiktas. In thirty games, he scored twice. Silkman aided the sale to Turkey. He explains, "Alex was back over, this time the club wanted to get rid of him as quickly as possible. Their attitude was, 'Please get him out', which is what we did by finding him a move to Besiktas, and once again, all his family were involved in the move."

Before United signed him there was reported interest from Barcelona and Leeds, but the player opted to stay at Paranaense because he was waiting for his girlfriend to turn sixteen so he could marry her. He eventually joined United for £6.5m, the first Brazilian to sign up at Old Trafford. Kleberson claims he was 'tricked' into signing for United by Ronaldinho. He said, "I was with the national team in France for the FIFA Confederations Cup. I can remember it clearly, I was with Ronaldinho and his brother/agent, Assis. Ronaldinho said, 'They want to sign both of us', so I said, 'OK, let's go, then!' I was so glad that he would be coming with me. I went back to Brazil and kept negotiating with United, but then Ronaldinho fooled me and went to play in the warm weather at Barcelona! He sent me to Manchester. That's a joke between us until today. He knows that he owes me one."

Zahavi tried to bring Ronaldinho to Old Trafford. Silkman worked closely with Pini in the Israeli agent's early days. Barry takes up the story, "I was at Manchester City when I first met Pini, when he was a football reporter in Israel. He took me from City to Maccabi Tel Aviv on loan, and that was Pini's first deal. He told me he earned more from that loan deal than he did in an entire year working as a journalist. I met Pini at the Leonard Hotel in Seymour Street in central London when he came over from Tel Aviv. I introduced him to many managers over here and that started his incredible career. But he promised me so much and didn't deliver, he must owe me £1.6m in commission, and as you can imagine we have fallen out over it."

Sir Alex described Mino Raiola as a 'S***bag' and 'a t***', which led Paul Pogba to leave for Juventus on a free transfer. Sir Alex saw huge potential in the Frenchman and was desperate to retain him, accusing Raiola of engineering the exit. In his book *Leading*, Fergie distrusted Raiola, 'from the moment I met him.' He added, "There are one or two football agents I simply do not like. And Mino Raiola, Paul Pogba's agent, is one of them."

Raiola responded, "Maybe Ferguson only likes those who obey him. From his quotes, I understand that Ferguson still doesn't have a clue who Pogba really is. Ferguson was an excellent manager, but the greatest managers can be wrong sometimes." Raiola took £40m to bring Pogba back!

Jerome Anderson told me, "I was introduced to Alex through my very close friendship with Charlie Nicholas when Alex was still manager at Aberdeen. Charlie mentioned to me that he thought I should meet the man who would one day become a very successful manager south of the border. He was right. The first time I met him I came away with a feeling that this guy was very passionate about the game. It was a very warm meeting, and we talked about many aspects of football. Alex has become a great manager in England because he brought his expertise from Aberdeen and he has such vast knowledge of the game. His commitment to Manchester United is unflinching."

Anderson developed a professional relationship with Ferguson. "In his early days we dealt with Lee Sharpe and Russell Beardsmore on Alex's go-ahead. He knows we do a good job with these players, although we did cross swords on just one problem that occurred with Lee Sharpe. Lee wanted to play abroad, and he asked us to examine the possibilities for him. There were people at that time interested, but they asked him to put his name to an agreement, a sort of confirmation that he would be interested. When Alex found out he wasn't amused, to say the least – that would be the best way of putting it. With Alex you know exactly where you stand. What you see is what you get. I admire the unbelievable successes he has achieved at Old Trafford so you cannot knock his methods. He's a winner, an out-and-out winner."

Dennis Roach was once one of the top agents in the world, whose clients included Mark Hughes. He died aged seventy-nine in May 2019. Dennis once told me about his dealing with Fergie. "It has to be said that Alex and I have never been the best of buddies, although I don't know why. When we meet socially we get on fine but business wise it has always proved somewhat difficult. I think the problem dates back to when Alex first took over as manager of Manchester United from Ron Atkinson. At the time I had a very close relationship not only with Ron but also chairman Martin Edwards. Perhaps Alex thought it was probably too close."

Roach brought Hughes back to Old Trafford from Barcelona, and then eventually played his role in the sale to Chelsea. He recalls, "Mark had an offer of a five-year contract to sign for Bayern Munich after going there on loan, but it was at the time he was marrying his fiancée Gill. As he told me, it was his one opportunity of going back to Manchester United and he wanted to take it. For some unknown reason Mark seemed to rub Alex up the wrong way, although this is something that Alex always denies. Yet Mark always said that if Manchester United were to lose 3–2 away from home and he'd scored the two goals, Alex would have blamed him for the three goals conceded! I've come round to Mark's way of thinking when you look at the way that, over a period, he was left out of important games, and there were occasions when his absence surprised the pundits and experts. One of those times was in the Champions League game in Turkey when United lost to Galatasaray and Mark was left out when most people thought that game was made for Mark."

Overall, Hughes got on well with Alex, but there came a time when he felt he was not getting a regular place in the side, very similar to the reasons behind his move from Chelsea to Southampton. There came a point at Old Trafford where he felt it was time to move on. Glenn Hoddle made an approach and he decided to move to Stamford Bridge. "Manchester United had been very good to Mark with a testimonial, but he wanted regular football. To be fair to Alex and Martin Edwards, the club were terrific in assisting with that chance to move by asking only a moderate fee of £1.5 million."

One of First Artist Management's 'clients' was being snapped up from Middlesbrough – Gary Pallister. It was to become a benchmark signing – a record fee for a defender – but, as Jon Smith OBE discloses, it was even more significant than that for Ferguson. Jon tells me, "The final meeting to clinch the deal took place, of all places, in a windswept car park at the back of a pub at Scotch Corner just outside Middlesbrough ... It was a revolting day but for some reason this was the only venue that we all came up with to maintain a degree of confidentiality. Bruce Rioch got out of his car and Alex, Gary and myself got out of our car. Bruce Rioch came up to the three of us and the first thing he said as he pointed to me was, 'You can f*** off.' That's all he ever said to me in the entire transaction. I think Bruce had an aversion to soccer agents! He wouldn't deal with me throughout the weeks of talks and the only contact I had with his club was through his board of directors. But to Alex's credit, he responded on my behalf. He told Bruce, 'No, he's part of the deal.' It took three hours to thrash out the deal. Gary desperately wanted to sign for Manchester United, but Boro were holding out for a massive fee at that time.

"When it was all finished, Alex put his arm around my shoulder and confessed that he felt that a record £2.3 million for a defender was a huge gamble. At that time the money was huge, and the reaction massive. He said he had put himself on the line. 'I don't believe I've paid so much for him,' he told me. He was really reluctant to pay that much but it was the only way to get the player he really wanted. Alex went on, 'If I get this one wrong I'm for the chop.' At the time his team was not doing all that well, and he knew that signing Gary Pallister was a big, big risk for him. It's ironic that Alex spent another record fee on another centre half when he bought Jaap Stam from PSV Eindhoven for £10.75 million."

Jon Smith OBE ran the Manchester United's 'players' pool' for the FA Cup final with Crystal Palace – a critical time for the United manager as this was to be his breakthrough trophy. Jon recalls, "This was the turning point for Alex, and I was with him all the time in the build-up to the final. There was no question that his job was on the line again. Danny McGregor, the commercial director, turned to me when United won the replay and said, 'That's it, now we're going to be successful.' From that moment Alex and his team never looked back and nor has the club."

Jon experienced the Ferguson mood swings. "Yes, Alex can be very unpredictable. One moment he is sweetness and light, the next moment he can explode over the smallest thing. The Manchester United team were billeted in the Burnham Beeches hotel, in preparation for the FA Cup Final with Palace. The sponsors wanted one final picture on the day before the big game. The team bus arrived back at the hotel after training and the photographer was waiting outside the hotel for his picture. The players accommodatingly got off the bus and were ready for the picture shoot. But not Alex. He was supposed to be in the picture, but he wouldn't get off the bus until he had finished his game of cards! When someone went on the coach to ask him to come off he snapped, 'No, I'm not ready.' Alex stayed on the bus playing cards with some of the players and wouldn't let them go until he had won his hand – no matter how long it took or how long everyone was left waiting for him. We all had to wait for twenty minutes. Finally, Alex disembarked from the coach, having won his hand. Now he was all sweetness and light."

Smith has nothing but admiration for the way Ferguson once ruled the Old Trafford dressing room with a rod of iron, "He is very authoritative. There is a commanding air about him. I really have enjoyed working with him over the years, and I have learned an awful lot from him, particularly how to deal with people."

Keith Gillespie couldn't believe how Sir Alex told a 'white lie' to get him a massive pay rise when he left United to join Newcastle as a £1m makeweight. Sir Alex secured a five-fold pay-rise in the £7m deal with Andy Cole arriving in a package deal. Gillespie was a teenager earning £250-a-week, when it came to finalising his personal terms Fergie shocked him by taking control of his wage demands. Keith saw Sir Alex as, 'A scary manager but scary in the right way.' What surprised him was how much he cared about his players, especially the young ones, and how protective he could be. Gillespie recalled, "You knew where you stood with him. He was fantastic for that group of players in bringing them through. He knew how many sisters you had, what school you went to, your mother and father's names. He sort of took the time to know all that."

Keith tells me, "I was at Manchester United for three-and-a-half years, starting out as an apprentice and growing up with that Class of '92, Beckham, Scholes, Butt and the Nevilles, but I wasn't a regular, so didn't always even train with the first team, so didn't get to know him that well. So, it was a surprise to me that he negotiated my contract when the time came for me to leave Old Trafford, I didn't have an agent, and he effectively acted as my agent! It all happened after an away game at Sheffield United. We got to the hotel where Sir Alex told me of the proposed deal and that Andy Cole was coming to United, and that we would be meeting up with Freddy Shepherd and Freddie Fletcher [of Newcastle United], it was around midnight.

"The first thing that Sir Alex said to me was, 'Get your mum on the phone' but there were no mobiles back in those days, so I had to call her from the hotel lobby phone. Sir Alex took the phone and asked her, 'Is it okay if I can act as your son's agent? I will have your best intentions at heart.' She was happy with that. Sir Alex was always very protective of the young players especially, and along with Beckham, Scholes, Butt and the Nevilles, we had all signed professional at the same time, and he didn't have us on big money, probably more for our own good. I was

£250-a-week, not big money. We were sitting at a big round table with Sir Alex, Kevin Keegan, Freddy Shepherd, the chairman, Freddie Fletcher, the chief executive. Sir Alex had a pen and piece of paper in front of him. I remember Sir Alex saying, 'Well, Keith is on £600 a week at the minute and we want you to double it to £1,200.' I had my head bowed when the meeting started but at this point I lifted my head, but Sir Alex stared at me, it was a look that said, 'Don't say a word.' Sir Alex was fantastic. They agreed to it straight away. It was just a little white lie and Newcastle may have been willing to pay it anyway, but Sir Alex was fantastic in the dealings. He also told me to think about it, and that I could have stayed, but I knew there was Andrei Kanchelskis in front of me and having a great time in the team, I wasn't a regular, and here I had the chance to play for Kevin Keegan, so I took it. Also, in the end he had got me five times the amount I was earning at United, so I agreed it straight away.

"He did ring me six weeks later, because he wanted to buy me back! Andrei Kanchelskis had left the following summer, but I was now in the Newcastle team, and happy to stay there. I wonder if he would have negotiated five times my salary to go back... I doubt it!"

Gillespie was once caught red-handed by Sir Alex buying drinks in a hotel in the early hours. "It was in the hotel where I had bought some drinks and was carrying them over to the sofa area, which was about ten yards away but just around a corner, and as I approached the sofa, who was sitting there? Yes, none other than Sir Alex. I was amazed he was there at that time, and he just stared at me, and I stared back. I turned round and legged it. I've no idea to this day why I legged it, because I wasn't doing anything wrong. It was a Friday night before a game, but I wasn't in the squad. I was just eighteen, doing what most eighteen-year-olds would do, but I never saw him again the next day, nor on the Sunday, but when I reported for training on the Monday, Brian Kidd came down and said the manager wanted to see you. I knew what that was going to be about. The Boss told me he was fining me one week's wages for telling the truth and two weeks for the lie. I told him I didn't lie. He responded, 'Two week's wages.'

"I didn't ever suffer the famous Fergie 'hairdryer' although I wasn't there an awful long time and wasn't involved in the first team too much, but if ever I was going to get the hairdryer, I thought this was going to be it. But it didn't happen. He was actually OK about it, apart from the fines." Gillespie went to the bookies to place bets for Sir Alex! "Back then, the gambling side of things wasn't a taboo like it is today. On a Friday, he would call me up and say, 'Can you put that on for me?' I was hoping it would win because he would always throw me an extra few quid if it did."

Sir Alex described dealing with Spurs chairman Daniel Levy as, "More painful than my hip replacement." United paid £30.75m for Dimitar Berbatov from Spurs in 2008 with twenty-year-old Fraizer Campbell moving the other way on a season-long loan. Sir Alex said, "Daniel Levy, chairman of Spurs, nailed us to the flagpole in 2008 when he took us all the way to the last day of the transfer window before agreeing terms for Dimitar Berbatov, Tottenham's talented Bulgarian striker in whom we had long had an interest. When we got wind of the fact Levy was trying to sell Berbatov to Manchester City, we stuck in our oar, chartered a plane and flew the player to Manchester, agreeing on terms with the player and, as I thought, a transfer fee with the club. Then Levy came back to us and said he needed Frazier Campbell, one of our young strikers, as part of the deal. David Gill demurred, so Levy then upped Berbatov's transfer fee a little. Finally, in order to get the deal over the line, and to add insult to injury, we sent Campbell on loan to White Hart Lane and paid the increased fee. We were up until midnight signing and faxing papers to make sure all the paperwork went through before the deadline expired."

The Treble

With a mobile phone that chirps 'Scotland the Brave,' it took a Scot to give English football one of its finest moments in club football, beating the Germans of Bayern Munich with two goals in injury time in Barcelona to land an historic treble. Caught by a television interviewer, Fergie's spontaneous response to the shock in the Nou Camp was a simple, "Football? Bloody hell!"

The registration number on Sir Alex's car spells out the word 'FAN'. He has as much passion as the most passionate fan. Sir Alex describes the 1999 Champions League final as "Without a doubt, my greatest moment as a manager. The stirring comeback against Bayern exactly epitomised all my teams. All the qualities that got you there in the first place came out that night – never give in".

In his first season after joining from Aston Villa, United hit the jackpot with Dwight Yorke. Sir Alex observed, "In my time, there was maybe Dwight Yorke who gave an immediate response. He was fantastic from day one. They are not always like that; he was an exception." Dwight tells me, "Sir Alex was an incredible manager to play for. He was an outstanding manager, but on top of that he was also a father figure, a helping hand when you needed it most. When you had a problem or an issue, he was the one you could turn to for help. He went far beyond the usual stereotype manager, he was a better manager than that, because he would be willing to help you with problems outside of football. It was unusual in football for a manager like him to take so much pride in making sure his players were alright both on and also off the field, and he did that so you could perform to your maximum. That made him outstanding on top of his ability as a manager and it brought the best out of his players.

"I can look back and reflect on how that worked for me, from the first moment I walked through the door, I was a marquee signing, the club's most expensive, but he went out of his way to take the pressure away and that was embodied by making me feel relaxed by telling me to put to one side the expectations because I wouldn't be there if he didn't feel I was good enough to be at a place like United. His kind words resonated, when he told me, 'Go out there and express yourself, you have earned the right to be at a club likes this, there are great players around you, and all of this gives you all you need, a great platform.' That is how he presented it to me, and I did just that, went out and played and expressed myself. I might not have appreciated it as much as I do now when I look back and can see how he made that big transition so much easier for me, it helped me be successful."

United landed the treble in Dwight's first season, he adds, "It was quite astonishing, and it's only now, during the pandemic, that I have had time and the inclination to look back, no doubt because, like everyone else, I had run out of ideas of what do after watching millions of hours of Netflix. There was time to reflect, and the treble was one of those moments in time that there was never anything like it then, or since. Taking that step back and reflecting, I can say that at the time I never imagined the impact it would have on our lives. I can walk down any street in the world, and I travel quite a bit as an ambassador for United, and people will want to talk about the treble. It still resonates with them, it was an iconic time, a piece of history. There is actually no word to describe what happened, the feeling then, and even more so now, the accomplishment was incredible, and no other club in Britain has been able to emulate it. It's such a rare moment in the history of the game. Quite astonishing."

Yorke asked Sir Alex for a twelve-month sabbatical, with full pay as reward for winning the treble! Dwight tells me, "I was very much a single man and that didn't follow the manager's guidance of wanting his players to be settled, family men. Instead I was a naughty little kid in a candy shop having lots of fun, winning Player of the Year, top scorer. Once in a while I got my wrist slapped. Looking back I understand now even more so than back then, why it was done for my own good. When you are in that bubble you don't think that the older generation understand, and you feel hard done by when he's so hard on you."

Rio Ferdinand joined United from Leeds in a world-record fee at that time for a defender. On his first day at the training ground, he hung around with Dwight – which earned him a warning. "I went into the training ground," Ferdinand said, "and Dwight Yorke, who had won the treble a couple of years before was on fire, him and Andy Cole up front. I walked around the training ground on my first day with him and I remember walking upstairs and Sir Alex Ferguson walking out of his office. He saw us and went, 'Alright, boys. Good morning!' We both said, 'Morning', me and Dwight Yorke. I had breakfast with him [Yorke]. [We] went out onto the training pitch and as me and Yorkie walked out, he [Ferguson] called me. 'Rio!

Come here.' It's like the headteacher calling you at school on your first day. I walked over and he went, 'Do you want to be here for a long time?' I said, 'Yeah, I want to win everything, and I want to do it as well as I can, boss.' He said, 'Well the first thing you should probably think about doing is not hanging around with him because he ain't going to be here.' Wow. I said, 'What?' He explained, 'He was unbelievable. He won everything but [he's] complacent now.'"

The current relationship between Fergie and Dwight? "It's amazing," Dwight tells me. "Last time I texted him he invited me out to lunch. When I told him I wanted to go into management he gave me a letter of recommendation which I have to this day. He sends me a card every Christmas. I didn't take in everything he said to me back then, I wish I had. But I am aiming to go into management, and I will take so much into it. He always told me, 'Don't lose your focus, or it will all pass you by.'"

After winning the FA Cup final against Newcastle in 1999, Sir Alex told his players, "Put your medals away, there is more to do" as the squad's coach pulled up at the Royal Lancaster Hotel, where families waited to celebrate. They'd already partied after lifting the title the weekend before. Next morning, United travelled to Bisham Abbey in Buckinghamshire for light training, before Concorde flew them to Barcelona for an epic final.

Before every European away fixture, there was a very heated players versus staff quiz. Steve McClaren recalled, "I remember one question about the artist of a famous painting. The gaffer said, 'The players have no chance here.' Nicky Butt answered it correctly, at which point the gaffer threw a knife or fork at Butty! And then accused John [the cameraman quiz master] of cheating! 'There is no way that Nicky Butt from Manchester can know who the artist is.' Nicky said, 'Yeah, I do know it, gaffer. I've got the painting in my dining room!'"

Bayern believed they had all the answers in the Nou Camp until substitutes Teddy Sheringham and Ole Gunnar Solskjaer delivered the most amazing finishes to become one of the greatest teams as Ferguson emulated Sir Matt on what would have been his ninetieth birthday.

Sheringham tells me, "People ask me all the time about Sir Alex, what is he like, what kind of coach? It's interesting because he wasn't a coach, he put on four sessions in four years. He left it to his coaches like Brian Kidd and Steve McClaren. Man-management was his main asset, he made everyone feel comfortable, he'd ask about your family, ask about your life off the pitch, he wanted you to feel part of it all. It worked, it made you able to concentrate on what happens on the pitch. Of those four sessions they would have all been before big European games because he would want to get his message across personally.

"I was thirty-one, a little older in my career when I arrived at Old Trafford, so I didn't really need advice, but he gave me some anyway when I first joined, not that I was asking. He said, 'I'll tell you something, son, you won't believe it playing for Manchester United.' I told him, 'Well, I have played for Tottenham, for England all around the world.' But he was right. It only took me three months to find out he was right. I had never experienced anything like it at Millwall, Nottingham Forest, Spurs, that teams would be happy to take a point from United, and if there was five minutes to go and it was 0–0 they would be delighted to hang on, and so too would their supporters.

"There were times when he would call me into his office an hour or even fifteen minutes before the start of a game. I was keen to play but I was kitted out as one of the substitutes or left out at times. I would go to see the manager in his office, and he would start to explain that he was resting me, but I would say, 'What do you mean resting me, I've only played two games, so I can't understand why you are leaving me out, because I'm not tired, I don't need to be rested.' Also, I said, 'There are big games coming up and I would want to play in them.' He looked at me, and told me, 'OK, I'm leaving you out, you are not playing.' He tried to put it nicely, but when I questioned him, he told me I was dropped and that was it. I never, though, suffered his 'hairdryer' but at different times I was sitting next to Ryan Giggs and Nicky Butt in the dressing room when they got it full blast. I sat there thinking, 'f*** me, hope it's not me next.'"

For Sheringham the treble was the pinnacle of his career, as he told me, "It's got to be. Winning stuff like that in football is just the best, unbelievable. It finished off an amazing eleven days in winning all three trophies, something you couldn't write, extraordinary, incredible to have been a part of it, something when you are growing up as a kid in love with the game you can only dream about."

For plain old Alex Ferguson, an appointment with the Queen and a knighthood at Buckingham Palace awaited. "How did we win that match?" Fergie would say, "Will somebody please tell me, 'cos I'm bloody sure I don't know. We earned it a sight more than they did. But I'm buggered if I know how we did it. There was all that talk about the treble, month after month of it. Suddenly it's there and you're trying to believe it. Then the thought strikes you that you've got to try to win it all over again next season. Christ, that'll be hard. All those extra matches, bigger demands, people trying to knock you off because of what you've done. Aye, very, very hard. I won't be saying that to my players, mind. When I get them back after the holidays, I'll say, 'Right, are we ready to go again?' And I won't be needing an answer. After this, we'll be playing for our pride, our place in the history of the game. There's important things at stake. My players will understand that.

"There were all kinds of omens about it. It felt like it was meant to be. The fact that it would have been Matt Busby's ninetieth birthday. The fact that we were playing Munich, with everything that name means to Manchester United. All that type of thing. I kept hoping it really meant something. People who believe in God might see a pattern in that. I mean I believe, I pray a lot. You have the sense that it all has a meaning. But, in the end, the most important factor was the spirit of the team. They just don't give in, they don't know how to give in. A manager can talk all day about tactics and preparation, but if the players can't bring the inner beast out of them then he's wasting his time. Well, they've got that beast inside them. And they found it when it mattered.

"A pal of mine came over from Australia for the game, but I couldn't promise him a ticket. So he watched it in London at some corporate function. Five minutes from the end, they all left the television room and went into dinner! Can you believe that? They heard my pal jumping and screaming and they all went back. One lad, supposed to be a United fan, actually missed both goals. Serves him bloody right."

Ferguson was thinking of Matt Busby. "There was all this din and chaos in the dressing room, then Bobby Charlton came in and we went over to a corner and poured a drink and we toasted him on his birthday." Ferguson was deep into the mental process of preparing himself for defeat. "I was reminding myself to keep my dignity and to accept that this was not going to be our year after all. I was not going to get myself twisted inside about it because I've got a life to live."

He admitted, "You can talk all you like about tactics, but tactics didn't win that game. It was sheer will. Maybe luck, too, but mostly sheer will. The players never stopped believing, and you have to give them credit for that. Bayern will accept it, I'm sure. We just never stopped. Our will-to-win gets fiercer with every game. The point I made to the players before they left the dressing-room in Barcelona was, 'You're playing a team who are not as good as Arsenal.' And Arsenal are better than Bayern, but I had to do that because the Germans have a similar mentality to an English team.

"Martin Edwards told me Beckenbauer gave the impression of being uneasy during most of the match. He was apparently agitated, as if he felt that something was not quite right, that they were going to lose. Naturally I was resigned to losing when we reached injury time, but once we equalised I didn't think they had a chance of holding out over another half hour. They were absolutely gone. Although you have to assume that if one of those efforts that hit the woodwork had finished in our net we would have been buried, I didn't think they deserved to beat us. They didn't commit their whole hearts to winning the game. We know we didn't play well by our standards. Losing a goal after five minutes in a European Cup final was bound to have a derailing effect. We did settle about fifteen minutes into the game and managed to get it going for longish periods, but the application of quality wasn't constant. At half-time I used what Steve Archibald told me when he came to see me on the Tuesday evening – the worst part of his experience of losing a European Cup final with Barcelona was at the end when the Cup was only five or six feet away and he couldn't touch it. I asked our lads to think about how they would feel if that happened to them. It was a simple bit of motivation, but it stressed the gulf between winning and losing in a match like that. I was moved by how emotional Steve Archibald was when we won. When he played under me at Aberdeen, our relationship wasn't always cosy, but I liked the lad, always felt a lot of warmth for him. Seeing how he reacted really increased my pleasure in the greatest occasion of my career."

Continuing at the time Fergie observed, "As I say, it wasn't anywhere near our best performance of the season. Against Juventus in Turin and in the two FA Cup semi-final matches with Arsenal I thought we outplayed our opponents. We didn't do that in Barcelona, but some of the stuff written about how Bayern outplayed us was weird. So were many of the assessments of Beckham and Giggs. Beckham was the star of the midfield show and Giggs worried them plenty. The finish was quite simply unbelievable. We have some spirit as a team. And some substitutes! Sheringham and Solskjaer have done a fantastic job for us this season... He has such quick feet. That last chance couldn't have fallen to a better man."

It was also the area which caused Fergie most concern before facing Bayern, with Keane and Scholes suspended. He changed the team because of Beckham's display in the FA Cup final, when he switched to the centre of midfield from the right after Keane's injury. "My original intention was to play Ryan Giggs there," said Fergie, "but Beckham controlled the cup final and, with him in the centre, I knew our passing rhythm would be maintained. I decided on the Saturday night after Wembley that Beckham would be in the centre. Next season we've got Keane, Scholes, Butt and Beckham I can use there, but maybe we still need one more."

It was a passionate half-time speech in the Nou Camp dressing room by Ferguson, who sent his players out for the second half with the words "Don't come back here if you haven't given your all" ringing in their ears. Introduced as a sub mid-way through the second half, Sheringham recalled, "The manager just said, 'Go out there and get us a goal.' But he kept me waiting for a couple of minutes on the touchline. I don't know how long he thinks I can last these days. It was going down from twenty-three minutes to about twenty, so I said, 'Come on, get me on now.'"

Ferguson declared, "They're the best bunch of players I've ever had. They're a terrific team but they also play the right way and try to win matches, and you can't deny their attitude and will to win." Ferguson appeared at the after-match party. He sat outside on a first-floor terrace, "I hope that part of the result of that is that twenty years from now, when they talk about the chief characteristic of this particular team, they'll always be remembered for their last-minute goals, for never giving in. The 1968 side were men of their time and now my team cannot be ignored. They are men of their time now. I mean, two goals in injury time, who would have thought it? Maybe we were meant to win it. Maybe there was an element of destiny. With Matt's birthday and Bayern Munich all in there, I kept hoping there was a meaning to it. You could tell Matt was looking down on me."

When the conquering heroes returned to Manchester, there were an estimated 750,000 jubilant fans, providing an unforgettable welcome. They received an amazing ticker-tape reception in the city centre. Fergie raised a fist in triumph as he displayed the trophy. Ferguson hugged wife Cathy and said, "It doesn't get any better than this."

To relax he went to Pontefract Races to watch a horse in which his wife had an interest. "They gave me a great reception. Even Leeds fans were shaking my hand. Incredible! Still, there's been terrific warmth throughout the country. No question about that. It just shows how a bit of success can lift people. It's like England winning the World Cup. Great events make their mark." Ferguson continued, "It's strange to watch teams develop. The United side of '94 was full of strong people, strong personalities: Robson, Bruce, Cantona, Hughes. They influenced other players with their strength. This team has developed along those lines, and that same strength is coming out. Keane, Stam, Schmeichel – they influence people. David Beckham influences the game. Eventually, he'll influence the others. And then we'll have some player, won't we!"

Gary Neville reflected, "How many managers would have sent Peter Schmeichel, the world's greatest goalkeeper, on holiday to Barbados halfway through a season, allowing him to miss a Premiership match against West Ham? I don't think there's a manager around who would have the bottle to do that, but he did, and he's reaped the rewards. He's in total control of situations like that and I'm not the only one to benefit. He's absolutely brilliant in terms of giving the players a rest. He gives you the maximum time and doesn't say, 'I want you in – or else.'"

Sir Bobby Charlton led the chorus of praise. "This has been a sensational season," said Sir Bobby, a member of the 1968 European Cup-winning side and a United director. "It's been marvellous for the fans – the FA Cup, the Champions League and our own championship. And the players have just been great. I'm really proud of them. English football has been in the wilderness for a long time and now we're back on the world stage. It's alright saying English football is the healthiest and the best to watch, but you really need to have something to show for it and to win the Champions League, there's nothing bigger in world club football."

Willie Miller, Ferguson's captain when he managed Aberdeen added his congratulations, "I'm delighted for

Alex. This is a huge milestone for him. I think, if there was one trophy he wanted to win this season, it would be this one, but to complete the treble in the manner they did is quite astounding. Alex showed again he is prepared to make tough decisions like bringing on Sheringham and Solskjaer in the heat of the game. That's what sets him apart."

Once, when he took his endlessly patient wife to Rome for a romantic weekend they ended up going to watch Lazio. "Cathy takes it all in her stride," said Sir Alex, "but she was very relieved when it was over. The stress builds up in her because she knows how it's building up in me. Then she puts it out of her mind. On Thursday morning she was in the hotel in Barcelona, worrying about luggage and checkout times and all kinds of stuff. And I said, 'Hey, I'm standing here with a European Cup medal round my neck. Have ye no noticed it?' Ach, she takes no notice."

Ferguson reviewed the season, "The League was the thing. We knew we had to win that to make everything else possible. But, in the last stages, I wasn't feeling too well. I'd picked up the virus that went through the team. I kept feeling a bit low, a bit tired. And then, just before the game at Tottenham, it seemed to go away. I remember Dwight Yorke looking at me and saying, 'You're better, aren't you? You've started moaning at us again. It's all gonna be all right now.' And it was. It really was. We got that trophy in the cabinet. We used the FA Cup final to work on a few things, then we were off and running to Barcelona. Yeah, everything was alright."

Prime Minister Tony Blair personally approved the top gong which was formally announced in the Queen's Birthday Honours list on 12 June 1999. The Queen sent him a personal message following United's triumph in Barcelona, "Congratulations on your splendid win last night. It was a magnificent achievement, rounding off such an unforgettable season for you all." Tony Blair – a Newcastle United fan – said, "The whole country, whatever team they support, is absolutely thrilled."

Rangers' chairman, David Murray paid Fergie the ultimate tribute, saying, "There is no doubt he is the greatest manager of his era." Actor Richard Wilson – appearing in Manchester – forgot his grumpy Victor Meldrew tones and quipped, "A knighthood? It should be a sainthood." Rod Stewart said, "Of course, Alex Ferguson should get a knighthood – he's Scottish! He has done a fine job."

Ferguson said in an interview with the LMA's *The Manager* magazine, "I prefer to think about what's ahead and what I can achieve next, and I think that has kept my feet on the ground quite well. I've never got carried away with it. My wife, Cathy, is fed up with the whole thing. When Alastair Campbell phoned her about my knighthood she said to him, 'Do you not think he's had enough rewards?' You'll not find a thing about my career in the house at all. She's unbelievable. I can't even take a football book home, or she'll say, 'What are you doing with that?'"

Make Mine a 'Fine' Bottle of Red Wine

Sir Alex has a fascination with fine reds. Not just the Red Devils! Rival managers made it a point to order the very best bottle to entertain Sir Alex after matches. Sir Alex only had to quit alcohol for a time when recovering to full health following brain surgery.

Fergie is an avid wine collector – a passion that first began during an away trip in Montpellier. His interest sparked when he discovered bottles from d'Yquem and Pétrus at Montpellier's Maison Blanche hotel in 1991, while scouting opponents in the European Cup Winner's Cup that United went on to win that year. He says, "It was a time in my life when I needed an interest. My wife said I was becoming obsessed with the game. I wasn't a drinker, really. When I went full-time into football I didn't drink. When I got older, I used to take a sweet sherry. That was my drink when I was about thirty, and then I started taking a glass of red wine at about thirty-two. I remember my [wedding] anniversary, at about thirty-three, and I bought a bottle of wine for £15. I brought it home and my wife Cathy said, 'How much did you pay for that?' I said, 'Fifteen pounds!', she said, 'Are you off your head?' And then things progressed. When I went to Aberdeen [in

1978], I developed a more discerning taste in red wine. Then you progress to the level where I am now, to meeting this chap in Montpellier."

In the interview with Decanter, he divulged that he had around 800 bottles at his Cheshire home and many more in storage in London and Oxford, "My favourite drinking wine is [Super Tuscan] Tignanello," he revealed. In mid-2014, Christie's auctioned hundreds of bottles from his cellars making around £2.5m. His favourite tipples also include Californian Cabernet, Australian Shiraz and Ribera del Duero, a region he discovered while travelling Spain to scout a potential player.

Not so much white wines, "I've got a lot of Bâtard-Montrachet at home, but it never gets used. If I was at a big dinner I wouldn't refuse it, but I find a lot of white wine too acidic." Sir Alex opts for Bordeaux when dining in restaurants, preferring wines from Pauillac and St-Julien if available, "And of course, Pétrus, but that's a wee bit expensive."

He studied wines and his introduction to classed-growth Bordeaux was dominated by his desire to invest. He remembers the hotel owner in Montpellier talking up Bordeaux's 1982 and 1985 vintages. In the 1990s, he became friends with wine merchant John Armit and dined with the critic Oz Clarke. "At first, I was buying all the recommendations, but they weren't really making money. So, around 2000 I concentrated all my money on big stuff, like Pétrus, Domaine de la Romanée-Conti, Lynch-Bages and Lafite-Rothschild." He has had an allocation of Pétrus and DRC every year since 1996.

Sir Alex once joked he needed to order a new supply of good red wine for Jose Mourinho's visit to Old Trafford when United drew Real in the Last 16 of the Champions League. The pair had a tradition of sharing a glass after their teams' encounters – though Ferguson described the first wine Mourinho ever provided him as being 'like paint-stripper.' Mourinho made amends with a £300 bottle of Portuguese red next time. Reacting to the draw Fergie told United's official website, "Well, it's the tie of the round. It's a great opportunity for our fans to see Cristiano again and also for me to meet up with Jose again – I'll need to order some good wine! José promised me Barca Velha and brought something different. I gave him stick for it, so the next time he brought Barca Velha."

Following Sir Alex's retirement he struck a close friendship with Mauricio Pochettino and went on to share a bottle of Brunello di Montalcino at a Mayfair restaurant.

In the summer of 2008, the then Burnley manager Owen Coyle needed a favour. He was completing his pro-licence and was in Switzerland for the European Championships. He was with Jim Fleeting and Martin Ferguson [Alex's brother]. Coyle recalls, "We chatted away, and I said, 'Martin, can you do me a favour and phone the top man? He has a player and I want to speak to him before anyone else.' So he phoned him and put me on, and I said, 'I need a favour. You have Chris Eagles and I think he'd be different class for me,' and he said, 'We are back training on 4 July, and we'll sort something out. I give you my word, but don't bother me before then.' Sure enough, 8.30am on 4 July, I'm on the phone and he said, 'You kept your word, but I'm taking him on a pre-season tour of South Africa because I need him. But, when we come back, if he wants to come to you he's yours.' He also made us a deal with what it would cost so the whole thing was only £1m. He then said, 'Don't bother me until I'm back, but we'll sort it.' I then watched every game United played in South Africa, and isn't he the top scorer in the tournament? He's playing out of his skin. I'm thinking, 'I'm not going to get him.' So the first day back I phone again, and he said, 'Aye, I was expecting your call, son. Right OK, everything I said before was agreed.' I told him that I'd been worried, and he said, 'I gave you my word. If he wants to come on board he's yours.' He was then great with me after that. When we won the play-off final to get promoted to the Premier League, he messaged saying, 'You were brilliant this year but remember when we come to visit I want two nice bottles of red for me and my staff.'

"As it happened, our first home league game was against United and we won. Despite that, he must have sat for an hour and a half after the game with me. The class of the man. I'm teetotal, and I'd said to Darren, who does the PR, to go get two nice bottles. So he spent £300–400, and I went to put the two bottles in the fridge. Thank goodness he was there, or it would have been spoiled. Sir Alex and his staff drank the lot, so it must have been all right."

Sir Alex's reputation as a wine connoisseur was intimidating for rival managers. England goalkeeper Dave Beasant told me, "I was at Fulham when we played Manchester United at Loftus Road, at the time we were ground sharing with QPR. Steve King was the manager, and he told me, as he would be doing the after-match press conference, could I look after Fergie. Fine. Well, not fine really. We set up the catering staff to provide the best bottle of red wine they could find in the ground. He came into the manager's office after the game, and we had a lovely chat, and got on very well, it was such a pleasure to talk to him about football, horse racing, all sorts. Just me and him on our own, plenty of general chit-chat. I poured him another glass of the red and we talked more about his love of racing, before he finally said he had to go and join his players on the coach. We had drawn 1–1, so he wouldn't have been happy with the result and the next week we were going to Old Trafford to play them in the FA Cup. As he left, he said, 'Send Steve King my best wishes, and see you next week... when you will have a decent bottle of red wine rather than that shit you got.' It all went well, you have to give the man total respect, but the worst thing about meeting him was clearly the red wine wasn't anywhere near up to his high standards!"

Nigel Atkins elevated Southampton to the Premier League when Sir Alex came calling for his 1,000th game. Nigel's coach Dean Wilkins, brother of Ray, was in the manager's office sharing a bottle of red with Fergie. Dean tells me, "Managers are always offered a glass or two after the game, some don't bother, but Sir Alex would pop in for a glass of red and he stayed with us for about twenty minutes, chatting about the game and different players. I noticed that a third of the bottle was left when he departed. It was such a significant occasion I decided to take the bottle home as a souvenir. My daughter put it in a wooden frame and had it inscribed with Sir Alex's 1,000th game and I've still got it. It's a nice little memory of such an important occasion."

Sir Alex is no different to most managers when it comes to their attitudes towards refs. Former FIFA World Cup referee Paul Durkin recalled a moment when even Ferguson was in a good mood with the officials when United won the championship at the Riverside Stadium in Middlesbrough in 1996. He told me, "Alex personally brought a bottle of champagne for the officials. He said everybody else was having some so why not us? He came into our room and simply said, 'Thanks very much.' No doubt he was happy because they had won 3–0 and won the League! Other than that, I've had little to nothing to do with him. I don't know the guy. Usually the managers bring the team sheets to the referee half an hour before kick-off, but Ferguson left that to Brian Kidd, so I don't really have a lot of contact with him – unless he talks to everyone else but not to me! Let's be honest about it – the only time a manager wants to speak to a referee is when he wants to moan and groan! However, he's not had too much to moan about to me – Manchester United have only lost once when I've been in charge! Although that was against Arsenal."

Snooker & Horses

Sir Alex's love of horse racing is well known, but his love of snooker? Paul Ince knows much more than anyone of Sir Alex's passion for snooker. He is the go-to guy Sir Alex calls for a game, as well as Ryan Giggs, according to some fascinating insights and anecdotes from Ince himself. Ince tells me, "As an eighteen-year-old growing up you would find me in in my early West Ham days at the Ilford snooker club, spending my days as a YTS boy fine-tuning my snooker game, I was pretty handy. When I was at Manchester United, we would often stay at Mottram Hall Hotel in Prestbury, in Cheshire, not far from Manchester, where they had two snooker tables in their Spa and all the lads loved to go in there for a game. One day, Sir Alex joined us and fancied taking me on. I gave him thirty start and he beat me. Well, I let him beat me – to make sure I was in the team that weekend! But he couldn't get over beating me, and was letting everyone know, 'I've beaten him, I've beaten him.'"

Sir Alex has a snooker table in his home in Winslow, where Paul and Ryan are regulars. Paul continues, "Sir Alex has always had this love for snooker, and he would text me and invite me around to his house for a game, and

Giggsy also goes round for a game. Of course I would kick his arse on the snooker table, but he would ring Giggsy and tell him that he had won. Giggsy would then call me and say, 'I hear you lost to The Gaffer.'

"'No, I always beat him at snooker!' Sir Alex would ask me to come round to his house to play snooker, and for me it is a forty-five-minute drive from Chester. So, to make the journey worthwhile, he would say, 'Let's make it the best of three frames?' Fine. And I'd also give him a twenty-point start for the first frame. No problem, I knew I would beat him. But it was tight at the end of the first frame with just the pink and black left. I potted the pink and had the black to win, with the black sitting invitingly over the pocket. So I'd say to Fergie 'I'll give you a fighting chance, I'll put the black in off five cushions.' I missed the black, but just. 'I won' he would announce. Yes, but as I told him, 'I could have potted that black with my eyes shut.' But that was my fault, he pointed out, 'You tried to be clever' he would snap back.

"No worries, it was the best of three frames, as Fergie wanted it from the start, and I would win the next two, no bother. 'Oh no,' piped up Fergie. 'It has to be just the one frame, as Cathy is calling me, there's a doctor's appointment. Cheers, Paul, I'm off.' Well, that was that, so I got in my car to head off back home but hadn't been driving for more than twenty minutes when I get all from Giggsy, 'You lost to The Gaffer, I hear.' Clearly Fergie couldn't wait to get on the phone to brag about beating me. 'You can't be serious, Giggsy' as I told him the full story, and told him I'd be back to take my revenge. As I said, 'Fergie is a f****** cheat!'"

None of that detracts from Paul's relationship with his former manager. "Sir Alex and I get on fine, despite the competitive nature of our snooker, and the fact that he is a cheating bastard! He called me just before he was taken ill, and we spent some time talking football. We still call each other regularly, and I would tell him I saw him on TV watching a United game in that ridiculous mask."

The business of being a winner was something Paul admired and appreciated, when he moved from West Ham to a United dressing room packed with opinionated characters and many tales of confrontation with The Gaffer. Ince tells me, "When you think about all the trophies Sir Alex won, all the success, he was clearly a great manager. He was THE greatest of all time. The biggest thing for me observing him was how he managed so many players, so many big egos, so many opinions and so many strong individuals. It was not easy, but he did it. I've been in management myself, and it is not easy to get everybody singing from the same song sheet, especially before a game when it matters most. In that dressing room was myself, Keane, Schmeichel, Robbo, Giggs, Cantona, Hughes, big, big personalities. Disagreements, arguments, rows, there were so many, but when it came to putting his team on the pitch his team were united in every sense. He would make sure whatever issues we might have had with each other, with the manager, with the world in general between Monday and Friday, by the time Saturday afternoon came around all of those issues were put to one side.

"Let me tell you something, Sir Alex was one of these people that when he spoke everybody listened. Even when I was a manager sometimes you would look around the dressing room when you are giving them their last-minute instructions and there is always one or two distracted, doing up their laces or fiddling with something and not paying attention. Footballers are funny creatures, you tell them so much between Monday and Friday about the preparation but come the match they've forgotten most of it. So it's important to get your message across in the final minutes before they go out. When Fergie issued his final words everybody was looking him straight in the face and were taking it all in, and in those three or so minutes the manager had the players' minds set right for the match.

"Don't me wrong, he would also go off his rocker at times, but overall he was the greatest manager of all time and had the determination and stamina to keep going and get the club's first title in twenty-six years, which in itself was an unbelievable feat, but to take it on from there, was simply incredible."

Paul has a personal Sir Alex 'hairdryer' favourite. He recalls, "Numerous players have been on the receiving end of the infamous 'hairdryer', and I am no exception, but I must say it was quite an extraordinary set of circumstances, even by Sir Alex's standards. But I must point out when I tell you this, that we are best mates again! We were playing Norwich at Carrow Road with the title at stake. Norwich were going strong, so it was a massive, massive game, and we beat them, scoring three times and playing exceptionally well. Three minutes before the end, I picked the ball up and thought I'd kill some time by going on a 'mazy.' I beat two or three, but as I went to take on the fourth, I lost it, they broke quickly and nearly snatched a goal, but there was no time left to recover even if they had scored. We all made our way back to the dressing room, all chuffed with ourselves, happy days, with us all giving each other high-fives. In walks Sir Alex, and as he comes through the dressing room door he goes absolutely bananas with me, 'Who do you think you are?' At first I had no idea who he was talking about, who he was talking to, he was just ranting away. Then he looks at me, 'You are not a winger, what are you doing trying to beat three or four men, that's not your game.'

"I hit back, I wasn't taking that, 'Are you taking the piss?' I lost it, 'Are you having a laugh?' I told him, 'We beat the team at the top of the table, and all you can do is have a little dig... go f*** off!' Well, as you can imagine, that didn't calm him down, it enraged him even more, much more, and Bryan Robson and Lee Sharpe had to come between us. We had started to walk toward each other, and the players watching it all thought there was going to be a ruck, we would come to blows, it was that bad."

One of the players in that dressing room who witnessed the scene was Paul Parker who says, "I recall one of the biggest bust ups I witnessed was with Paul Ince. And thanks for telling me Incie thinks it was at the end of the game, but my recollection was that it happened at half time. Incie came in and took off his boots, threw them to the floor, and said, 'That's it.' He wasn't coming out for the second half. Something had happened, been said, and he was so angry he wasn't going to come out for the second half, and the row got so heated that Brian Kidd got between them when it looked to get really nasty. We all went out for the start of the second half, leaving Incie behind with Brian Kidd, who had pacified him, and he did come out for the rest of the game. But the Gaffer doesn't bear grudges, and he came to the back of the bus on the way home and seemed in a good enough mood. I'm sure he gave Incie a cuff round the head and gave him a look as if to say, 'Well done' as we had won an important game, he wasn't ignoring him, and that was the end of it."

Paul and his teammates forgot about it and moved on. They had seen it all before, but for Paul Ince, it was a different matter. He feared the fall out would linger but he was shocked that it didn't. He went on, "I was dreading Monday back in training. When you got a bollocking from The Boss, especially one as bad as this one, you would fear that you would have a rough ride back in training that week, that the manager would be walking past you along the corridor and wouldn't say a thing. Training on Monday turned out to be a game of head tennis. But guess who decided to be the referee? Yes, Sir Alex. He hadn't said a word to me, he hadn't even looked at me but here we all were with the manager in charge of our game, and it was quite a game, one-all, two all, and so on until it got to ten-all and the deciding point. The ball was in the air and I hit a perfect overhead kick, over the net, and right on the line, the winning shot, and our team were going mad with excitement at our victory. Then, all of a sudden, we heard, 'Out'. The referee called it out! As we hadn't been speaking all day, I couldn't pipe up and say a thing. Everyone knew it was in, but Sir Alex called it out, so out it had to be, and we lost. There I was frothing at the mouth, desperately wanting to say something, but thought to myself, 'f***! I'm not giving him the satisfaction.'

"On the way back to the changing rooms, I heard the manager's voice bellowing across the training camp, 'Oi, Incie, there is only one Gaffer here, and it's not f****** you!' He wanted to let me and everybody else know who was Boss."

Horse racing was Fergie's main source of relaxation. "My father loved the horses." Ferguson once said, "But he was bloody hopeless at them. It got to the point where my mother used to maybe put a line on a Saturday and she would whisper to me, 'Find out who he's backing.' So I would go across and say, 'Fancy anything today, Dad?' He'd say, 'Two certainties.' He always said that. He said, 'I'm going to slaughter them today, slaughter them.' Then he'd tell me what they were. I'd go and tell my mother and she would put her money on something else. She'd back two others. Then there was this day when my mother had a yankee and the third one up came to the last fence and it was that far ahead that it was from here to Chester. Anyway, it jumps the last and it stumbles and falls. So mother goes, 'Blinkin hell.' She goes to my dad and she says, 'You didn't back that, by any chance, did you?' He just sat there, and he wouldn't answer because he was like that – none of your business sort of thing. And she just rounded on him and she said, 'You're a jinx!'"

Fergie bought Queensland Star, named after a ship his father helped to build on the Clyde. It won its maiden race at Newmarket, leading from start to finish. Queensland Star was the first to carry Fergie's red and white at the 4.45 with West Ham fan Gary Carter in the saddle and trained by Jack Berry near Lancaster. Another was Candleriggs, named after a district of Glasgow and managed by Ed Dunlop in Newmarket – and steeplechaser Yankie Lord, with Charlie Brooks at Lambourn.

Fergie once said, "I love golf, but I really enjoy racing and it's something my wife Cathy and I can do together. We went to Cheltenham on Gold Cup day and that really got us."

Sir Bobby Charlton at one time regularly played golf with him, "Quite frankly it's best if I don't say too much about his golf – it's pretty bad, really." Sir Bobby looked forward to his golf days with Sir Alex which was an opportunity for the manager to relax. "Sometimes you can get him out to dinner or maybe on to the golf course. And, really, he's quite pleased when people sometimes give him the chance to step away from it a little. But it doesn't make much difference. All he wants to do is talk about United. His mind is never off it. Yet these demands are not from the club. He puts those demands on himself. Despite his heavy schedule I believe he will never ever experience what you might call burnout. This is his life's work. It's what Alex Ferguson is all about. And I can see him just going on and on..."

It was his profound love of horse racing that got him into hot water in 2003 when Fergie began legal proceedings against Irish horse racing tycoon John Magnier. The toxic dispute which sent shock waves through Old Trafford concerned the horse Rock of Gibraltar. The Glazers control of United can be traced back to the row over the £200m racehorse and the power struggle that threatened the very core of the club. Such was the bad blood between United's majority shareholders and their manager that my sources told me, allegedly, that a private detective was employed to find out as much as possible about Ferguson that might prove useful in their impending court confrontation; the claim is totally unsubstantiated. My source has an inside track on what started the conflict, "Rock of Gibraltar was running at Warwick where, if it won, the owner traditionally made a speech, and John Magnier wasn't keen on a speech, and suggested that Alex Ferguson did it instead. Alex was happy to do it, but it was a speech made by the owner. So John wrote down on a piece of paper that Fergie owned a quarter of the Rock of Gibraltar. The horse won, and Fergie made the speech, and John thought that was the end of it. John thought it was no more than a bit of fun and giving Ferguson the piece of paper was all part of it. He thought no more of it."

Rock of Gibraltar turned out to be a world-beater, setting a world record of seven straight Group 1 race wins collecting more than £1.2m prize money. The big money-making potential lay in its stud. For Fergie, Magnier and his Irish racing partner JP McManus tens of millions were at stake. Fergie and Magnier were once close friends with a shared love of racing. "One of the reasons I like it is that people leave me alone for the most part," Fergie once revealed. "And when they do talk to me, it is likely to be about what is going to win the 3.30 rather than football."

On November 17, 2003, a statement issued on behalf of Magnier read: "Coolmore Stud has today been advised that legal proceedings have been initiated against Mr John Magnier by Sir Alex Ferguson alleging certain ownership rights to the stallion Rock of Gibraltar. Coolmore Stud and John Magnier consider the action to be without merit and it will be vigorously defended." My source went on, "When Rock of Gibraltar went to 'Stud' Ferguson produced the piece of paper which stated he owned a quarter of the horse, which he insisted meant a proportion of the stud rights as well. John Magnier told Fergie, 'Don't be so stupid, it was all a bit of fun.' But Ferguson didn't consider it a bit of fun. Not in the least, and that was pretty clear when he embarked on legal action. But he was dealing with some powerful people, and there was certain 'evidence' produced and when Ferguson became aware of the consequences of going to court, he accepted it was best to reach a settlement, take what was on offer, and that is what he did. The 'evidence' was pretty comprehensive, and parts of it, you would have to assume could only have been gathered with the aid of private detectives."

Magnier and McManus submitting the infamous '99 Questions' demanding answers from the United board over the club's affairs, finances and transfer dealings, including the transfers of Ronaldo, Jaap Stam and Tim Howard. They threatened to 'take action' against United if they were not given satisfactory replies. It forced an internal investigation into the dealings of Fergie's son and agent Jason, who was barred from representing further players at the club.

Magnier and McManus owned almost thirty per cent of the club and sold out to the Glazers. Fergie settled out of court for a one-off payment of £2.5m. Ferguson and Magnier agreed that neither would publicly discuss the finer details. In Ferguson's autobiography he said, "Rock of Gibraltar was a wonderful horse; he became the first in the northern hemisphere to win seven consecutive Group 1 races, beating Mill Reef's record. He ran in my colours under an agreement I had with the Coolmore racing operation in Ireland. My understanding was that I had a half-share in the ownership of the horse; theirs was that I would be entitled to half the prize money. But it was resolved. The matter was closed when we reached a settlement agreeing that there had been a misunderstanding on both sides. Obviously, there was a potential clash between my racing interests and the ownership of the club, and when a man stood up at the AGM and insisted that I resign, there was awkwardness for me. I have to say that at no point was I side-tracked from my duties as manager of Manchester United. I have an excellent family lawyer in Les Dalgarno, and he managed the process on my behalf. It didn't affect my love of racing and I am on good terms now with John Magnier, the leading figure at Coolmore."

Fast forward to Sir Alex's retirement and he 'scored' a treble when horses he owns won the first three races on day one of the Grand National Festival at Aintree. Looking toward Anfield, Ferguson said, "It's been fantastic, great.

Winning is the name of the game. Winning on Merseyside, they will all be happy over there. That's the best day I've had in my time in racing, which is about twenty years or so." Asked if he offered trainers advice, he said, "I don't interfere with the horses at all – that's the trainer's job. I didn't want anyone interfering with my job."

Hatred of the Media

Sir Alex made no secret of how much he detested the media. When asked by his close friend Alastair Campbell, he said, "Bloody nightmare. I think a lot of the live coverage of games is good and it's brilliant that every single league game is recorded on film. But the papers are a nightmare. They have all this space to fill, they're under pressure from TV and the internet, the journalists are on short-term contracts and worried for their future but so much of what they write is just rubbish. I tell you, the press in our country are a real problem. They do real damage. I kept saying to you, the government needs to do something because it's got worse not better." But even Fergie had to comply as he explained, "You have to. It's part of the obligations before big games. It's also a way of talking to the supporters, making sure they know what's going on. It's not a part of the job I particularly like, but you have to do it. I think it's fair to say you and I have reached pretty similar views about the state of the media."

Sir Alex ruled out punditry, "Not a chance. Some of the ex-player, ex-manager pundits are the worst. It's a disgrace the way they sit there criticising guys they used to play with, just to make a bit of an impact. I couldn't do that."

Privately, Sir Alex can be surprisingly compassionate, as he explained to Campbell, "You know my definition of friendship – the real friend is the one who walks through the door when the others are putting on their coats to leave. You had some pretty difficult periods, and it was important you understood there was support out there. I know from my position here that sometimes there can be so much noise and fury going on around you that you need people outside your own bubble who can take a slightly different perspective for you. We all need that."

Former Arsenal and Scotland goalkeeper turned TV presenter Bob Wilson experienced both sides of Sir Alex, "Appreciation of Alex Ferguson's talents comes down to his will to win. I've never met someone with such passion to be a winner. I would talk about Alex in the same breath as Bill Shankly and Jock Stein – that's all I can do. I got to know Shanks and he was the greatest character I have ever met. Jock Stein once gave me a bollocking but that's another story. Shanks was a great psychologist and Alex has a lot of that, too. I remember the day before the FA Cup Final. It was piddling down and when he saw me he said, 'Aye, Bob, have a good game tomorrow ... but the pitch will be a nightmare for goalkeepers.' Jock Stein had presence. Both of them were also winners, but I'm not sure they had bigger determination to win than Alex."

Commitment to the cause can boil over, as Bob tells me, "After a very confrontational meeting outside the visitors' dressing room at Highbury in 1988. I asked Sir Alex (or plain Alex as he was back then) to sign my book about Aberdeen when he had been manager. It never got signed but instead he was clearly upset by an interview

I had done the previous day on *Football Focus* with Liam Brady. He was so angry he actually pinned me up against the wall in his rage. During the interview that upset Alex so much, Liam was asked by me about the progress of United. He basically said they weren't like the Busby Babes going forward but was complimentary about Alex sealing up the defence with the signings of Gary Pallister and Steve Bruce. He was never critical in the true sense. Hence the quite physical confrontation the next day with me, the Arsenal goalkeeping coach! I wrote a letter to Alex and his response was quite breathtaking, quite something to behold and quite unexpected. Basically Alex was saying that as long as he was boss at United they would do it his way. However, it seemed to end any dispute.

Long-term following this I never had a problem either meeting him or interviewing him. In fact he was quite brilliant especially as he followed our daughter Anna's battle with her rare cancer. He always asked others of my ITV crew to leave us alone for these talks. Anna died on December 1, 1998 six days before her 32nd birthday. Three days later we received a call from Alex. He spoke to me for maybe five minutes and then to Megs for almost fifteen minutes.

"Amazing, quite amazing in his concern and humanity. After we launched our charity 'Willow' in Anna's name he has been supportive in every way with helping provide our Special Days for Seriously Ill Young Adults between the ages of sixteen and forty. Incidentally, more than 17,000 days have been delivered in the twenty-one years of the charity. This is one truly great man and more important human being."

Bob Wilson's letter to Alex Ferguson:

BBC tv

BRITISH BROADCASTING CORPORATION
KENSINGTON HOUSE RICHMOND WAY LONDON W14 0AX
TELEPHONE 01-743 1272 TELEX: 265781
TELEGRAMS AND CABLES: TELECASTS LONDON TELEX

26th January 1988

Mr A. Ferguson
Manager
Manchester United
Old Trafford
Manchester
M16 ORA

Dear Alex,

I would very much like to clear the air after the angry remarks you directed at me on Sunday at Highbury.

I would have liked to have done it there and then but felt it wrong to enter into an exchange in public.

Liam Brady, who has tremendous standing as a professional footballer, was asked to be a guest on Football Focus in the same way numerous players and managers have been before him. The programme is about the game and opinions held within it, but most of all, we like to think, it is always constructive not destructive.

If Liam's suggestion that, in his opinion, Manchester United seem to have moved away from flair players has caused such offence to you, I can only express real surprise.

It was simply an opinion from a player who has achieved an enormous amount. He also directed similar views on the Republic of Ireland, Arsenal and Juventus.

For you to say "Who is Liam Brady, what does he know about Manchester United was, I feel, insulting to him. I am also surprised you should choose to express yourself so forcibly in front of others. Surely it was a matter between you and me or you and the Editor of Grandstand.

Suffice to say I personally felt the attack was unfair, unwarranted and unbecomming the manager of Manchester United.

I only hope that it won't prevent my being able to approach you in the future.

With best wishes.

Yours sincerely,

(Bob Wilson)

cc: John Philips, Editor, Grandstand

John Motson has been on the receiving end of Sir Alex's Jekyll and Hyde character.

Motson tells me, "I remember when I was covering Aberdeen versus Liverpool in the European Cup in 1980. I had never met Alex before, but I phoned him up and told him I was doing the commentary for the English viewers and requested his help about his players. He made a special journey out to my hotel to help me out with the background on the club and his team. I thought then that he was a man going places with a sense for public relations."

Motson has not found Ferguson to hold a grudge, "When he joined Manchester United I had a lot of dealings with him, and I must say I have had a slight fallout on a couple of interviews. Once I asked him a couple of questions immediately after a match that were near the mark for him. He got just a little bit cross! But the next time I bumped into him, all had been forgotten." Memory man Motson couldn't remember the particulars of the after-match interview row, although it might well have been the occasion of a Roy Keane sending off.

Motson retains nothing but admiration for Ferguson. "Of all the managers he seems to be the one who is at his desk the earliest in the mornings. If you ring him at 8.30am you know he'll be there at his training-ground office." As for Ferguson's record, Motson adds, "How many men have won so many championships? Very few, apart from Jock Stein and Walter Smith whose achievements were all in Scotland. In modern times no one has won more championships on both sides of the border. What I admire most about him is that in an era when player power has taken over in a lot of places, he has remained one of the few strict managers in the mould of Brian Clough and Bill Shankly. Let's face it, that isn't so easy these days when the players are paid so much and can be millionaires before the age of twenty-one.

"I've also seen the other side of Alex, a hugely compassionate guy. He lost one of his real big mates in Scotland and he was really cut up about it. I'm sure it's his competitive edge that puts people's backs up because his attitude is all about winning, but there is a kind side to him that I've discovered because of my family problem. Every time I met him he would ask about Ann's health. 'I'd be saying a prayer for her,' he would say to me. That's all the more incredible considering that on one occasion he had some very strong words. However, Alex might give you a bollocking but the next time he sees you he doesn't ignore you. You can take his bollocking on the chin or finish up disliking him for the rest of your life."

The one-time owner of Crystal Palace Simon Jordan is now part of the media entourage on *talkSPORT*. Simon tells me, "We played United in 2005 and Sir Alex was not very happy, not happy at all, by the way his team lost at Selhurst Park. He kept his team waiting on their bus for forty-five minutes while he drank our best Scotch in our boardroom. I was pretty underwhelmed by that. As he was in our boardroom, we managed to have a chat, and he wanted to know a bit more from a personal level having met me, no doubt wanting to make his own mind up as he had probably heard about this very young brash football club owner, who back then had a bit of an edge about him. Most football club chairmen were a bit predictable back then, and are so today, but I was out there, and said it how I believed it and didn't pull any punches, happy to say what was on my mind. I am sure Fergie liked that. Twenty years on, I am a bit wiser and a lot older, of course, but the old me was much more robust and outspoken. But I don't recall we talked about anything much profound, didn't evaluate our philosophies, it was more about getting to know each other a bit more.

"His management style is very much seen as a product of his age, so much 80s and 90s, but I don't see it that way," says Jordan. "In fact I see it as the blueprint for management much the same way as you see it from the likes of Jose Mourinho and Pep Guardiola. While Jose lost his edge, Fergie never did. For me he was the greatest manager of them all, and only the likes of Mourinho and Guardiola for what they have won in the game come close. But Fergie had it all in management terms. I've bumped into him since, mainly social functions, but haven't really spoken, so you can say I have admired him from afar. I am not one of those people who glad hand others, so I would leave people alone, but I heard a great deal about him from Brucie [Steve Bruce] whom I employed as a manager, and there was no doubt the respect Brucie had for Fergie. He loved him. It was good to get an insight into Fergie from him, someone who respected and revered him as a manager There is no doubt that since Fergie left the dugout and David Gill left the boardroom, Manchester United have not been the same."

Trevor Brooking met Fergie and was impressed by his off-the-field demeanour. Trevor told me, "The only time I've seen him in a relaxed mood was when he came out for the Italy–England game in Rome and we were in the same hotel reception before the big match. It was the first time I had seen him in an environment when he was not thinking about participating in a game and he looked extremely relaxed. I've heard he has a good sense of humour and the people he trusts see a different side to his character and personality than the one generally given to the public. He is also a very loyal person. You can see that when he is intensely protective of his players and the club in general."

Brooking has no doubts about Ferguson's pedigree, "Yes, I would say he must be regarded as a great manager. I don't think there can be any real question about that. He transformed both Aberdeen and then Manchester United. I think that Manchester United were a massive club that were underachievers and are now a financial empire with fantastic foundations for continuing their success. The strength of their youth structure makes them a magnet for all the best young talent throughout the country."

Trevor doesn't underestimate the importance of discipline reflected in the way that Ferguson insisted his players looked whenever they travelled abroad, "All the players dress and behave in a correct manner, and I feel that says a lot about the discipline within the club and that the manager places an importance about how his players appear. The way the players look reflected the authority that Ferguson exercised within the club. I would go as far as to say that the Manchester United players and club are the most impressive travelling group from this country."

Brooking doesn't disagree that a great deal of the lack of popularity for United stemmed from the manager, "It is a shame if it is the case that the club's unpopularity among rival fans stems from the manager. Perhaps Alex does need to loosen up now and again! Unfortunately Alex is a public figure who has a poor public image to a certain extent. There is an element of Alex begrudging opponents' success; he can come across as a dour individual. I find it all very strange for someone who supposedly is so experienced with the media. He could handle the media a little bit more affably than he does. All right, we live in a world that rewards winners. Alex is a winner. He has got all the plaudits he deserves for his achievements, and he has been a winner because of that outward intensity. Yes, at times Alex's attitude works against them. Of course, there is always a lot of envy around when any club is successful."

Andy Gray once dared to suggest live on Sky Sport that United won penalty favours from referees. Sounds familiar. This particular accusations dates back to the time that Gray and Richard Keys were the faces of Sky. Andy didn't quite allege that Sir Alex's teams won penalty favours from the officials, but that's how Sir Alex interpreted it. The result was a TV row. Gray told me at the time when viewers still wrote letters, before emails, "Alex should actually see my mail that arrives at Sky from others around the country who think I'm so biased towards Manchester United that I shouldn't be doing the job. I can see what Alex is saying, but it was my opinion, and he might not agree, but it won't be the first time Alex and I haven't agreed."

When Andy felt Barnsley deserved a penalty against United, he said so, but then he suggested that had it been an appeal for a penalty by United they would have got it. Andy told me, "What can I say about Fergie? Well, the Barnsley game just about sums him up. I was analysing the game afterwards when I said what about ninety-nine per cent of the viewers were no doubt thinking anyway – I wondered if it had happened at the other end whether Manchester United would have been given a penalty? What I didn't know was that as soon as the game was over Alex went straight from the touchline to his room, switched on the telly and heard my analysis of the penalty. That's Alex for you – damn thorough. He doesn't miss a thing. So, when he was being interviewed, he was armed with every fact about the penalties awarded to Manchester United in all his years of management. In his interview he told everyone that he thought my comments were utter rubbish and that Manchester United had had so many penalties in his time and it was no more than average, and it was ridiculous for me to suggest otherwise. Of course, I was unable to answer back so it was pretty frustrating for me."

Normally anyone who crosses Ferguson will receive a personal blast from the dogmatic United boss. Not Andy. He rang Ferguson the next day. He recalls, "Yes, we spoke the following Monday. I rang him and left a message that I wanted to speak with him, and he rang me back. I know what he's like, so I wanted to clear the air. He said to me, 'Listen, Andy, I'm passionate about the game, and you're passionate about football, and when two passionate people are involved there are bound to be disagreements.' That was the end of the matter – what had to be said was said, and there was no animosity. Unfortunately, in a newspaper article I made my comments about this incident, and the headline-writer, all credit to him, put up a headline that had nothing to do with my observations. Ferguson was none too pleased, and we had a row in the tunnel at Chelsea the next time he saw me. He had taken great exception to the headline and had a pop at me in the tunnel and I had a pop back. But the next time we met he was as right as rain. We acknowledge each other and pass a few pleasantries. We might not be bosom buddies, but I have a healthy respect for him and I am sure he has a healthy respect for what I try to do. I can say nothing finer about Alex Ferguson than that he is probably the greatest manager in English football since Bill Shankly – and that is saying something. What he has achieved at Manchester United is phenomenal. People talk about all the wealth at the club, but I don't think that is what is really important. On the playing side, in terms of success, he is on par with Shanks, who took Liverpool from the second division to the supremacy of the English game."

Sir Alex called Jimmy Hill a prat for having a go at Eric Cantona. One newsman accused Ferguson of inventing the word 'paranoia.' Jimmy condemned Eric Cantona for a vicious tackle on Norwich City's John Polston and Ferguson took enormous exception. Jimmy had no regrets about making his stand against the challenge which he felt threatened the career of a fellow professional. The often-controversial Hill made detailed references to this incident in his book, *The Jimmy Hill Story*. Jimmy declined an invitation from Granada to appear on a TV documentary about the life and times of Ferguson for a variety of reasons but stressed that none of them had anything to do with this incident. The late Jimmy Hill commented, "I say in my book that after the match Alex threw a wobbly and called me a prat after I described Cantona's tackle as wild and reckless, putting John Polston's future at risk." Hill and Ferguson had never discussed the issue since. Hill told me, "It's weird, we haven't met since and I suppose there has been no reason why we should. I do my work for the BBC in the studio and don't go to the grounds. I've been chairman of Fulham for the past ten years and in all that time we've never been drawn against Manchester United. I have seen him on occasions but never to chat to, and the circumstances have never arisen for that to have happened." So what would they have said to each other had they talked? "We would probably have a giggle about it." In his book Jimmy admitted to feeling 'shock and horror' by being described as a 'prat.'

Jimmy passed away aged eighty-seven in 2015. He was one of English football's most influential figures. When he worked for Sky I was privileged to have shared the round table with him on numerous episodes of *Jimmy Hill's Sunday Supplement*. I interviewed him about Sir Alex for one of my previous books back in 2000. Jimmy told me, "I have said in my book that I would never hesitate to condemn any tackle that might affect a player's livelihood, and I felt that this tackle did just that. It all happened a long time ago but it's an easy line for people to write about or even remember... oh, yes, Jimmy Hill's a prat, and it's something the fans can easily latch on to."

Hill told me, "At first Alex was never able to achieve any consistency at Manchester United and then the tongues began wagging. At that time I used to phone Martin Edwards from time to time. I am not suggesting that Martin faltered at all, but I emphasised my strong conviction that he would turn things around. It sounds silly that I should have had such faith, based on a three-hour acquaintance over half a bottle of Scotch, but nevertheless it is true. Consequently I rejoiced when he eventually did turn it around and things came good for Manchester United. He went on to become highly successful in such a short space of time that it defies belief. We all know that Alex has a temperamental, even tempestuous side to his character, and I don't think I mind that, so long as it is with other people – not someone who has been in his top ten supporters club!"

Hill put aside all his personal feelings to make as objective an assessment as he could on whether Ferguson is the best. "It is not really a question that can be answered. Someone like the manager of Port Vale has been a spectacular success in the light of the resources he has had and the pro rata kind of expectancy levels. It is much easier to achieve the kind of success that puts you in line to be the all-time best only if you are manager of one of the top half a dozen or so clubs in the Premiership. In my case I had five and a half years of total success in management, but no one rates me as one of the all-time best managers, and that has a lot to do with the club I managed, and the fact success didn't amount to winning the first division because no one really expected that was obtainable for that kind of club...

you can't win the championship in the third division! Alex Ferguson has done as well as I expected him to do from our very first and only meeting all those years ago in Glasgow. In fact, he's done even better. I am so pleased that the basis of his teams are English or at least British. He has used foreign players but only used them sparingly. For every foreign player he has imported he has brought on three potential candidates through the Manchester United ranks."

Genial Des Lynam made a chance comment that upset Fergie far more than he imagined. Des takes up the tale of the misunderstanding, "Alex did take me to task for supposedly telling him how to run his football club – as if I would try to do that. Let's face it, no one would dare to tell Alex Ferguson how to run his football club. Certainly not me. It was no more than a chance remark about the development of the young players at Manchester United at about the time that Ryan Giggs was still a teenager. I posed a question to Alan Hansen on TV, something like, 'Alex Ferguson does a marvellous job at Old Trafford, particularly protecting these young men from people like us. I wonder if it's time to take the gag off and allow a player like Ryan Giggs to talk to the media?' Alan Hansen's response was, I recall, brief but to the point and he suggested that Alex should indeed let the players off the leash.

"For some reason Alex interpreted that as telling him how to run his club. He certainly had a bee in his bonnet about it because a little later on in his video he responded to what I had said. It seemed to me that he had briefed the interviewer to ask him the question about my remark on *Match of the Day*. Alex responded, 'He's been trying to tell me how I should run my football club.' I was slightly amazed by it all, if not disturbed, to be truthful. I have spent my entire life in television without trying to put myself forward as some sort of expert, so it was very bizarre to say the least. I can only assume that Alex had got the wrong end of the stick and perhaps hadn't actually seen or heard what had occurred but had been told by someone. I conducted a face-to-face interview before the FA Cup Final and we spent a very pleasant time together, discussing the football issues over a glass or two of champagne. The subject of his displeasure was not raised. Had it been, I would have simply told him precisely what I've told you...'

Des and Sir Alex have no problems on a personal level. Des says, "We get on just fine. We are much the same sort of age. I'm a year younger than Alex, but we're of the same generation. I have a great regard for him. I have nothing but admiration for those who are not given the greatest hand of cards when they start out in life but deal with the cards they've got magnificently. I admire his ability as a football manager. He has undoubtedly proved himself the best in the business in recent years in this country. I sometimes find his public image comes across a little harsh and that is probably the reason why some people don't like him.

"Personally, I admire Alex for being himself rather than trying to be cosmetic, particularly in front of the cameras. Many people act out a role on TV and are something quite different off-screen. He doesn't bother. Alex has the courage of his convictions to be himself even on camera. He doesn't suffer fools and nor is he prepared to be overtly friendly toward the media or try to gain any special treatment from us. Direct. That's the best way to describe his attitude. I would certainly say that. It's a brave man who would tell Alex Ferguson how to conduct himself or to run his team. Sometimes it has to be done. But it hasn't been done by me!"

Chris Hollins is the BBC sports presenter who won *Strictly*. Son of footballing legend John Hollins. Chris tells me, "I've observed him in press conferences, and he is unique in the way he handled the media. He was unique as he was the only manager I can recall who didn't need or care whether he had the media on side. He was a formidable character whom the media needed more than he needed the media. It even left hard bitten, veteran, experienced journalists, in fear of asking him pertinent questions. There was a Champions League semi-final against Inter Milan, and the day before Roy Keane had said, 'If we don't win this game, there will be a major clear out among the playing staff.' Everybody wanted to ask Sir Alex the only question worth asking, about what Roy Keane had said. No one dared, though. They all knew he would bark at them, 'Stupid question, get out.' He wielded so much power.

"It reached the stage where all the British press contingent would brief their foreign counterparts, on this occasion, the Italian media, and at other times French or Spanish, to ask the tricky questions knowing that Sir Alex would probably respond and couldn't throw them out and not invite them back next time. Journalists needed access to Old Trafford press conferences, and Sir Alex would use this as a threat hanging over them. Sir Alex was an old-fashioned style manager, a throwback to the 80s. My dad played in the 60s and 70s when the players had to be on the right side of the manager, because they were earning £100-a-week, plus another £100-a-week when they played, so the manager could bark and scream and the players would take it, and respect him if they wanted to play and earn.

"The modern-day player is earning £100,000-a-week whether they play or not, in some cases, even twice that amount, and the role of the manager has changed but still has to motivate those players. However, there has been a major shift of power toward the players. Somehow Sir Alex managed to maintain his old discipline from the 80s on 21st century players who are global icons, without diminishing success, and they still had respect slash fear in every aspect of his management. One of his main gifts was to be able to continually reinvent teams at a regular pace and not lose that edge As for the media, as the decades went by, they had the same problems and often had to accept obtaining after match comments from MUTV, the club's in-house station, if the manager didn't feel like speaking to them."

Chris avoided 'hairdryer' moments but tread a very thin line on occasions. "I did ask him some intense questions at times, even knowing he might not be keen to answer them. You knew when he didn't want to answer, he just gave you that look, so you either got short shrift or he just ignored you. But as it was the BBC you felt you might get away with a bit more, but he would still snap, 'Silly question.' It was just a case of how brave you felt after that. Of course, then came Sir Alex's feud with the BBC, and while we still invited by the club the press conference, any hope of a one to one had gone."

Barry Davies knew, 'Quite a lot of people in TV did have issues with Fergie', but he didn't, at least, not too often. He tells me how Sir Alex was peeved that ice-skaters Torvill and Dean won a BBC award rather than his treble winning team, "It was an FA Cup match at Tottenham on a Sunday, when Alex had had a row with a chap from Sky the previous week. I was doing the commentary, and I was told that he refused to have any of his players or himself interviewed by the BBC after the match. I was invited to do something about it, no doubt because nobody else would dare! I went straight to the chairman and made it clear that while people know who he is, he is also an international figure and needs to make himself available or at least somebody else in his team. If his team wins today, he cannot deny the fans, the public, their expectations to hear what he has to say. Apparently, it was all about the BBC awarding Torvill and Dean their major award rather than United when they won the treble. Sir Alex changed his mind and came to do the interview, but I have no idea whether his chairman ordered him to. Later he refused to talk to the BBC in general over an issue, but he came out to see me after one match and said to me, 'I want you to know, it's nothing personal.' I'm told he said the same to Motty."

Keir Radnedge is one of the most respected global journalists. He tells me, "Sir Alex Ferguson's attention to detail has always been legendary. From the names of the staff behind the scenes at Old Trafford to the families of the myriad youngsters dreaming – usually, sadly, in vain – of a future in the limelight. That command of every aspect of the Manchester United machine was brought home to me in eye-catching and colourfully precise detail during preparations for a prestigious pre-season tournament at Old Trafford in early-August 2007. Argentina's Boca Juniors, Japan's Urawa Red Diamonds and PSV Eindhoven from the Netherlands were the high-class visitors for an event which demanded full focus from every aspect of the Old Trafford match operation. This included, naturally, the luxury restaurant facilities for visiting club directors, officials and those VIP guests who are always in evidence when Manchester United are playing at home.

"The company organising the tournament has commissioned my assistance with press promotion and publicity. Hence this role brought me to a watching brief for the discussion about the restaurant set-up – menus, numbers, tables and seating. Every point was meticulously noted and addressed by the restaurant manager. Right down to the specific cutlery and table displays. With very particular and deft handiwork she produced from her files an inter-leaving pile of napkins. The colour balance was exact: red, white, red, white, red etc. 'That,' she explained proudly and with a tone which brooked no argument, 'is how the manager likes them.' It was a perfect example of attention to every last, little detail – Ferguson style."

David Meek reckoned Alex Ferguson is the best of the seven managers he has been associated with. Meek, who worked with Sir Matt Busby, a great publicist, says that Ferguson gets the accolade because he was 'like a breath of fresh air' when he took over at Old Trafford. Meek, as a *Manchester Evening News* reporter for more than forty years, relished the fact that Ferguson was always sitting at his desk at the training ground every morning at the crack of dawn. "He was the Evening newspaper man's dream," Meek once told me.

He added, "He always kept me in the picture in time for the first edition. Having worked with a previous United manager who used to turn up for training at about 10.30am and would say, 'Nothing has happened yet today,' Ferguson showed he knew what it was all about. You can't ask for any more than that. He was always there when you needed him and always available and co-operative." David, once described by Sir Alex as, 'part of the fabric of the club,' died at the age of eighty-eight in October 2018.

In 1995, he earned Sir Alex's loyalty after supporting him at a time when some fans were questioning the manager's future. He defended Sir Alex during a controversial phone-in poll on whether Ferguson should be sacked. "The result of the poll showed a majority in favour of him going and I was asked to write a story accordingly," he wrote. "In fact, what I did was argue that if you deducted the votes of Manchester City fans wanting to cause mischief and you took into account the United supporters who couldn't be bothered to ring in, you were left with an overwhelming vote of confidence in Alex Ferguson. That was the moment I became a 'Fergie man', close enough to help write his programme notes for twenty-six years."

The day Ferguson walked through the doors of Old Trafford one of his first tasks was to acquaint himself with the local media. Tom Tyrrell was the Piccadilly radio football commentator, and his relationship goes back to Ferguson's first day at the club. He dealt with Fergie virtually on a daily basis. Tom has now sadly passed away. In my previous book on Sir Alex, Tom told me, "I interviewed Alex Ferguson on the morning he arrived at the club, the first radio interview he did, and I have interviewed him ever since on a regular basis. His record speaks for itself. He has equalled Sir Matt's record of five in 1952, '56, '57, '65 and '67. He has already won the FA Cup more times than Sir Matt. In my opinion, Alex was the best ever Manchester United manager. Sir Matt is The Boss – he was such a loving sort of person, while Alex was a totally different character, but even so he treated me like his nephew and has always been very, very good to me over the years, although he never gives you any clues about his transfer targets. I once said to him that Manchester United ought to try to be like Southampton in the way that they signed Kevin Keegan without anyone knowing and they just unveiled him at a press conference when they whipped back the curtain and there he was. I think he liked that idea. But I do feel the club's public relations could have been much better, and their relationship with the media could have improved if they had somebody from the media taking on that task."

Tom knew Ferguson as well as anyone in the media. He once told me, "A lot of people don't know the side of Alex where he has such a tremendous sense of humour. He can be a practical joker as well. I asked him to join in one of my jokes on 1 April. At the time there was a huge debate about the merits of artificial surfaces – it must have been back in 1987 – and at the same time the club were having enormous problems with the Old Trafford playing surface. I came up with this practical joke about how Manchester United were to resolve their problems with the pitch with a revolutionary plastic one. I conducted a mock interview with Alex where we both ended up in fits of laughter which I had to later edit out. He took it a stage further and said on air that Manchester United would be installing a synthetic pitch and it would be a red one! He said that the plastic pitch had been perfected by Swedish scientists and that the 'grass' was the closest to the real thing. Alex also said they would have illuminated goalposts, which would flash whenever anyone scored! On the air we actually had an interview with a Swedish scientist, talking about the synthetic surface. That night on *BBC North*, the regional TV programme, they showed a picture of Old Trafford with the playing surface red! It was the best April Fool's joke we have ever pulled off – it was a real cracker. Whenever I think of an April Fool's joke, I think of that one.

"He got me to interview a young Manchester United player and he wanted me to be particularly hard on him for some reason. He wanted me to put the poor kid on the spot, and to ask him pre-arranged questions while Alex and his assistant Brian Kidd were hiding in a position where they could hear the boy's answers. I really put the lad through it, trying to keep a straight face."

Tom was the victim of a Ferguson practical joke when he asked the manager's permission to interview Ryan Giggs after he starred in the Youth Cup final of 1992 but United had just lost the championship to Leeds after losing at

Liverpool. "I stood in the corridor with my microphone in my hand, but I hooked it under my strap. Alex had agreed that I could do the first interview with Ryan Giggs. George Switzer, who played in the Youth final at full back, one of the boys who didn't make it, came down the corridor and stood beside me in his shirt, shorts and socks, and was on tiptoe talking into the microphone. I said, 'Alright, George, it was quite a good game.' He said, 'Yeah, it was a fantastic game.' I suddenly realised what was going on. Fergie and Kidd were like the Marx brothers with their heads popping round the corner with Eric Harrison joining them. I had asked to interview Ryan Giggs, but they had sent out George instead."

But it was not all laughing and joking with Ferguson. Far from it. "I've faced his wrath on a few occasions," said Tom, "but each time I felt I was the innocent party. Although he will blast off at you, the next day you can be best friends again. It's usually a case of a misunderstanding as far as I'm concerned. The first time, he accused me of always being at the club. I was there doing a phone-in programme. But I was always at the club, and he knew it, and had never objected before so I couldn't quite understand that blast. I put it down to a 'bad hair day.' I was the one around the place and he picked on me."

Tommy Docherty was an outspoken critic of the team, of Ferguson, particularly in the early stages of his management, and had written something that Alex clearly didn't like in a newspaper article. "At the same time he was working for us at Piccadilly Radio. It reached the stage where the players refused to speak to us and Ferguson made reference to this in the press room where everybody heard it. A couple of the national papers picked it up, asked me about it and it appeared in the press the next day. I was asked, 'You would think Manchester United was bigger than this, wouldn't you?' I replied, 'Yes.' Unfortunately it turned out that I was quoted as saying, 'Manchester United should be bigger than this.' When you fall out with Ferguson you have to sample 'the hairdryer.' It was coined by Gordon Strachan. Alex Ferguson puts his face right up to yours and shouts – it feels like a blast from a hairdryer! I was on the receiving end on another occasion when there was yet another total misunderstanding. Eddie Booth used to work in the Old Trafford press box for the best part of a generation, a lovely old guy who I used to help out on occasions.

"I put out a story for the Press Association on one of those times I was helping out Eddie. It concerned Ferguson's complaints about the Christmas fixtures when Manchester United had to play at Chelsea with a noon kick-off on Boxing Day and then away to Southampton on New Year's Eve. Ferguson had said that they hadn't really considered the fans, although it didn't really matter to the players and to himself because they were used to being away over Christmas and New Year. He was more concerned about people like myself who had to drive all the way to London early in the morning for the early kick-off on Boxing Day and then drive to Southampton and back on New Year's Eve. The story was given a twist by the newspapers that Alex clearly didn't approve of and blamed me for it. It was reported that a whinging Ferguson wanted to cancel Christmas football.

"When he caught sight of me at Stamford Bridge he let rip. This was the only time when someone saw him having a go at me. I said to Alex that it would be better if we sorted it out outside. It must have sounded as if we were going to have a fight, which, of course, was not the case. The next day he invited me into his office, we had a cup of tea and sorted out our differences. It's never pleasant, having a row with anyone, but one of his strengths is that he doesn't do anything devious because he has fallen out with you. It's always up front and instantaneous, shouting and screaming, but then it's finished. I've always been a United fan and held the United manager, whoever he is, in high esteem. I've got to know them over the years, and you find out they are only human after all, with their own peculiar frailties and nuances. In fact, they are really like everybody else. I have always got on with Alex, and it's been no problem."

Dennis Signy, OBE, former editor of the *Hendon Times* and close friend of Margaret Thatcher, met Ferguson in the dressing room on his first day in charge at Old Trafford. Signy once told me, "From that day to this Ferguson has been a friend to me and is completely different to his public persona. He is charming – he carried my wife Pat's bags to her car after a function in London – and humorous. He is a family man who can switch off from football when the occasion demands. As a football manager he ranks among the top of the greats I have met in my fifty years in football. His success at Manchester United speaks for itself.

"He has always been co-operative and has been conscious that the image of United is correctly projected. When Eric Cantona was controversially chosen by the FWA as the Footballer of the Year, I rang Alex and expressed concern that Cantona might not turn up because of the adverse publicity he had received after the Crystal Palace incident. Alex replied, 'He'll be there.' Enlisting the help of his secretary he organised a car from Manchester to the Royal Lancaster hotel in London and travelled down with him." Dennis was the doyen of football writers. Dennis sadly passed away in June 2012 at the age of eighty-five. He was a mentor to myself as a young football reporter making his way in the often brutal world of Fleet Street."

Gary Newbon recalls how Ferguson, at the faltering start of his United dynasty, first saw red when as an eager broadcaster he dropped in a probing question over rumours of his impending sacking. Gary tells me, "He didn't like that question. But to be fair, why would he? He told me that the next time he wouldn't be giving me an interview. But I hold my hands up and it was a touchy question with so many rumours flying around, so you can see why he took offence. However, we sat down to thrash it out and I told him that I was probably out of order and that, if in future, I had a difficult question, I would be fair to him and let him know I would be asking it before I put the question to him. He was fine with that, and we had a good relationship after that."

Gary recalls an incident as United landed the treble, "When Fergie took his team to the Nou Camp for the Champions League final against Bayern Munich aiming to land the treble, I was the ITV regular interviewer throughout that tournament. I had been doing after-match interviews with Fergie throughout at the rounds leading up to the final. But this was going to be quite different because the Nou Camp in those days had a small dirt track between the spectators and the playing field, and an enormously long tunnel. I had real problems with UEFA that day as they were insistent that they would not be allowing me access anywhere near the pitch. The best I could negotiate was that they would let me watch the match pitchside, but they refused point blank that I could do any interviews pitchside, and because the tunnel was so long, I foresaw major issues once the game was over.

"United were losing 1–0 to Bayern Munich but in the stoppage time, later known as 'Fergie Time' Manchester United staged one of the most exciting ever comebacks when they scored twice and extraordinarily actually won the final that they looked like losing. Now came the hard part, to get hold of Fergie for the big after match interview, but I managed to head him off down the long tunnel, but because it was so long, I was beginning to lose radio contact and feared it wasn't going to happen.

"I managed to get the interview. Fergie was as good as gold and more than happy to be interviewed by me live. However, it didn't turn out how I had expected. I'd say he was in a state of shock – his mind had gone blank. I looked at him, he was just smiling at me. I asked him an easy question, can't even recall what it was, but it was short and simple, nothing too testing or controversial, just wanting a quick soundbite comment to reflect the enormity of the occasion. But he didn't answer the question. He shook his head and said, 'Football, bloody hell.'

"I had a very brief chat with Alex next time I saw him, after his book had been published and I tried to persuade him that his comment was actually an epiphany that has gone down into legend, as one of the all-time memorable quotes. I am sure I got that interview on such a special occasion because of my relationship with Sir Alex that had grown over many years and had been based on trust. It is all about trust when it comes to Alex's relationships with the media, and just about everyone and everything else. His problem with the media down the years is that he walks into an interview room and there is so much media there, that he doesn't know who half of them are and what their agenda might be, which always puts him on his guard, and he comes across as frosty.

"Very few see the other side of Fergie, the soft side, the caring side. Instead they have an impression only of an abrasive character, but there is another, a great side to him that people don't see or understand. To have survived that long as Manchester United manager in such a tough world of management, you have to be tough and single-minded. When I was very ill, after I had a stroke, and was admitted to hospital, Alex was on the phone to see how I was and to wish me well. When my wife suffered a brain tumour, he was back on the phone to see how she was and how I was coping. I was in hospital for a week with my stroke, and fortunately had speech therapy that worked straight away, but besides the call from Alex, I had letters from Brian Clough, Alan Green and Mike Ingham who was kind enough to say that I had inspired him to become a journalist. I also had calls from Terry Venables, Trevor Francis, David James and all sorts of people in the industry. But the call from Alex was very special and I will always remember that act of kindness."

Sky Sports' long-serving after-match interviewer Geoff Shreeves is writing his own book the same year as Sir Alex turns eighty, and, hardly surprisingly, he tells me that he will be dedicating an entire chapter on their numerous exploits. Geoff was on the receiving end of the 'hairdryer' on more than one occasion as he told me, "He always tried to do things the right way, and in the right style. He was one of the best. I've been on the touchline for thirty years and I can tell you I've interviewed a few in my time, but he is the best interviewee I've ever had to this very day; he always gave you something. He would prefer to be challenged, but only in a respectful way. He didn't want you to go looking for a cheap headline, nothing irritated him more. All the time, though, he spoke with enormous passion. And if he was not happy with you, he would let you know…"

Sir Alex was infuriated with Geoff's line of questioning after United beat Middlesbrough in December 2006. Ronaldo tumbled inside the area despite Mark Schwarzer failing to make contact, and Ferguson told Shreeves to 'f*** off' after being asked about it. Geoff experienced many heated moments, no stranger to experiencing Fergie's darker side, but by far the worst came at The Riverside. It threatened to get out of hand in the tunnel when Fergie came after him physically, but never got there as people jumped in. Geoff later patched up his differences and accepts he might have actually been in the wrong. "Fergie was in the right and I was in the wrong and I addressed that with him. We sorted it out very amicably, very quickly and it was never mentioned again."

Shreeves reflected on the mind games used by managers, for which Ferguson was notorious, during their matchday press duties. "Managers use us. Fergie was the master at it, not just reflecting on the game, but to send a message to their players, to the board. I have fond memories of numerous occasions involving Sir Alex. Yes, some of those include my run-ins with him, and I am sure when you google them, as I am sure, you have done, there will be plenty of detail. But what you won't find on google is that he has been a guest at my charity events. He has been a good friend, and that I have nothing but admiration, respect and fondness for him."

Sir Alex's 'First' Retirement

Sir Alex opted to 'retire', then suddenly changed his mind. The United board's decision to appoint Sven-Göran Eriksson as his successor triggered the U-turn, according to one conspiracy theory. Not so, says the man who knows. That's Pini Zahavi the agent who brokered the deal that would have taken Eriksson from the England team to Old Trafford. According to one of my sources, Sir Alex feared that his great legacy would be under threat as Sven had all the credentials to rake in a haul of trophies once Sir Alex departed. Eriksson accepted the position of United manager and had even signed a contract.

My source told me that Fergie had got wind of Eriksson's appointment. "Fergie feared that Eriksson, who was on top of his game at this stage of his career, would be a huge hit at Old Trafford and would win up so many trophies that Fergie changed his mind and wanted to stay on as manager."

From his home in Tel Aviv, Pini informed me, "When Sir Alex decided to quit the club were looking for somebody to replace him, of course, and they had decided to take Sven. I was involved and we almost closed the deal, but then Alex changed his mind." As for the conspiracy theory that Sir Alex got wind of the deal and performed his infamous U-turn, "Not so," insisted Pini, "his family made him change his mind, they told him he was too young to quit football entirely. They told him to stay in football, and that was the reason. It had nothing to do with Eriksson. In my view, Sir Alex did not know that Eriksson was even a candidate. It was only afterwards that he found out."

In his autobiography, *Sven: My Story*, Eriksson wrote, "I had a contract with England until the 2006 World Cup and I would be severely criticised if I broke that contract. But this was an opportunity to manage Manchester United. A contract was signed. I was United's new manager. One day I got a phone call from Pini Zahavi. He wanted to know if I could come for breakfast at a club in London the following morning. He did not want to say on the phone what it was about. It was very secretive. 'Sure,' I said, 'No problem.' When I arrived, Pini was there with Peter Kenyon, the chief executive of Manchester United. Straight off the bat, Kenyon asked me did I want the job as manager of Manchester United as of next season? I didn't think about it, 'Yes,' I said, 'I do.' I would be able to stay with England through the World Cup. My appointment would not be made official until after the tournament.

"A contract was signed – I was United's new manager. A couple of weeks passed and Pini called again. He wanted another meeting. When I got there, I knew something was wrong. Kenyon explained that Ferguson had changed his mind. He did not want to leave the club after all but had agreed to stay in the job for another three years. I don't know why Ferguson had changed his mind. In the papers they wrote that his family thought he would miss football too much. Maybe his U-turn had to do with United's relatively poor season. Surely Ferguson did not want to leave his career on anything but a high. I know that he was made aware that the club had picked me as his successor. Had he vetoed my appointment? It did not matter. He kept his job and I kept mine. But to this day, Pini has the signed contract where it says I was Manchester United's new manager."

Eriksson crossed swords with Fergie but also retained his enormous respect for him. Again in his book, he writes, "Sir Alex Ferguson was a genuinely nice man. We met many times and even had dinner together on a few occasions." Eriksson knew that anyone who 'bothered' Fergie in any way would face the 'hairdryer'. Erkisson knew Sir Alex, 'Would not spare his venom' especially with England managers. Eriksson described how Ferguson 'caused a fuss' before virtually every England friendly as he considered friendlies 'completely useless', a hinderance to his preparations for games, a source of concern about injuries, "Sometimes Ferguson would call at seven o'clock in the morning, ordering me not to select one of his players for a friendly. The player was injured or else he needed to rest, Ferguson claimed. I was not going to let Ferguson bully me. If I wanted a Manchester United player in my squad, I was going to select him."

Sven recalls the FA's anti-doping team turning up at United's training camp to conduct tests on four randomly selected players, amongst them Rio Ferdinand, who missed the test. Chief executive, Mark Palios, instructed Eriksson not to select Rio for the decisive Euro qualifier in Turkey. Ferguson called Eriksson, 'at the crack of dawn.' Eriksson wrote, "He wanted me to select Ferdinand in the squad, directly disobeying the order I had been given by my employer. 'I can't select Ferdinand,' I said. 'You have to call and yell at someone else.'" During this conversation with the irate Fergie, he couldn't help think just how close Sven came to replacing him at Old Trafford!

Eriksson had no problems with any of the club managers, except Ferguson, who defended United's interests, 'at any cost'. Eriksson, though, admired it, "It was a good trait to have, but it made my job more difficult." Eriksson's biggest 'scrap' was before the 2006 World Cup in Germany. Chelsea played United, 3–0 up with ten minutes to go. The match was over, yet Rooney threw himself into a tackle, coming off in agony. The England team doctor, Leif Swärd, was at the game so Eriksson asked him to check on Rooney. When Ferguson saw Leif outside the dressing room, he pointed at him and said, "Don't let him in."

Rooney had broken a metatarsal, just as Beckham had done before the 2002 World Cup. Later, Fergie called Eriksson, "You can't pick Rooney for the World Cup."

Eriksson, "Who says that?"

Fergie, "My doctor. Rooney is injured."

Eriksson, "OK. Then I will come with my doctor to talk to you."

They met Ferguson and United's doctor at the United training ground. Rooney cannot play in the World Cup, Fergie was issuing a directive, not a request. The United doctor had X-rays that showed Rooney's broken bone would not heal in time. When the doctor finished, Leif asked, "Why do you sit here and lie to me?" Eriksson recalled, "I thought Ferguson and his doctor would fall off their chairs. I almost fell off my own chair. I had never heard Leif even raise his voice." Leif told them that he had operated on similar breaks and did not accept their assumptions. Eriksson added, "I just wish I could have filmed Ferguson's face, and his doctor's when Leif explained that Wayne's break would heal in time for the World Cup. Maybe he would have to miss the first game, but he would be ready for the second, no problem. When

Leif had finished, I turned to Ferguson. 'Sorry, Alex,' I said, 'I will pick Rooney.'"

Before selecting his squad, Sir Alex called, screaming into the phone about making his life difficult if Rooney was selected contrary to his wishes. Eriksson simply stated, "Alex, I wish you a very nice holiday, but I am going to select Wayne Rooney for the World Cup. Goodbye." Eriksson hung up. It was the last time he spoke with Sir Alex during his time as England manager.

When Sir Alex finally did quit, David Moyes was assumed to be his recommendation, but he sounded out alternatives. Carlo Ancelotti spoke of how Sir Alex approached him but committed himself to Real instead. Ancelotti said, "I can say that I keep a fantastic relationship with Sir Alex. We met when he decided to stop but I was close to Real Madrid. I appreciate the fact at that time he talked to me. I've had no other opportunity to manage them."

Fergie approached Jurgen Klopp when he was manager at Dortmund. Klopp was reported as saying, "Alex and I have contact, He texts to say, 'This is my new number' and I take it as a big honour. We have a really good relationship. We were friends from my point of view working together for something good and on Sunday, he wants Manchester United to win, and I want Liverpool to win. That is possible and still be friends."

They joined forces for a fundraiser for the Alzheimer's Society. Klopp believed it is impossible to emulate Sir Alex. "I don't think it is possible anymore to be honest. Other clubs didn't have United's combination of an exceptional manager and squad at that time but now a lot of clubs are similar. I am sure Fergie didn't say at the beginning he'd win it thirteen times. He did what he did and made good decisions."

The Inside Stories

Sitting in the Sky studios commenting on Manchester United's victory parade and the Final Fergie Farewell, it struck me that, just like his favourite crooner Frank Sinatra, would we ever see a Sir Alex comeback? The party was over, it was time to call it a day. His resignation in 2013 sent shock waves throughout the footballing world, prompting statements from the Prime Minister, politicians, and celebs. The then manager of Norwegian side Molde, Ole Gunnar Solskjaer, told MUTV, "I will never forget the loyalty he showed me. Everything I have learnt I have learnt from The Boss." David Beckham reacted, "As I have said many times before, The Boss wasn't just the greatest and best manager I ever played under he was also a father figure to me from the moment I arrived at the club at the age of eleven until the day I left. Without him I would never have achieved what I have done in my career. He understood how important it was to play for your country and he knew how much it meant to me. After 1998 without the manager I would have found it virtually impossible to cope with the attention I was getting on and off the field and for this I will always be grateful to him for his support and protection. I am truly honoured to have been guided by the greatest manager in football and to have had the career that I had under him. Thank you, boss, and enjoy the rest!"

At his final press conference, Sir Alex was applauded into the room and given a bottle of wine and a cake, presented by *The Sun*'s Manchester correspondent, Neil Custis, banned by Sir Alex more times than anyone else! Not the usual tea or coffee at the training ground, but wine, served in plastic cups at 9am. At his previous press conference, Sir Alex poured champagne for the media to celebrate the 20th League title and then suggested the Greater Manchester Police would be waiting with breathalysers at the end of the single-track road that leads to the Carrington training complex.

Presenting the cake, Neil said, "It's been a rollercoaster ride and it mirrors Manchester United for all of us. There have been highs and lows, but I think when Sir Alex has been on form with us anywhere from Carrington to Kansas, from Turin to the Temple of Doom he has brought drama, he's brought colour to our pages. When he's been on form it's been gold. He has left us with phrases that will go down in the annals, and he has left us all with squeaky bum time on occasions! In years to come all of us will look back and feel privileged that we did this job at a time when this manager was manager of this football club, and for that, we thank him."

Sir Alex commented, "Dealing with the modern media is difficult for managers and I've been lucky that I've integrated into all the different stages in my time here. It got me in a position where sometimes I don't accept what you write and sometimes when you write nice things, I tend to dismiss it also. I've always thought you've had a terrible job, a difficult job with the pressure you're under with modern television, the internet, Facebook and all the rest of the nonsense. But I've never held grudges. Even when I've banned people, I don't hold grudges as it's not my style. I react and then forget about it sometime later. Thanks for the kind words, Neil, it was very good of you, and thanks for the time I've had here.

"Thirty-nine years as a manager and from that day staring at East Stirling with eight players and no goalkeeper to today six keepers and about 100 players, if you count the academy. I remember the old chairman, he was a great chain-smoker. I asked him for a list of players he had and he started to shake, his cigarette was going 100 miles an hour. He gave me a list of eight players with no goalkeeper. I said, 'You know it's advisable to start with a goalkeeper.' That was an education that. It was fantastic. Anyone starting in management should start that kind of way, but I don't suppose it is that way now.

"I'm driven to take on some challenges and some other things right away. I've got the League Managers' meeting on Monday, Newmarket Tuesday and Wednesday. I'm going on holiday, it's the Derby on 1 June, then the operation, then the recuperation, then the season starts. It can't be a substitution, it's a different life. People used to say to me, 'Do you think this one will be a manager or manage United?' about players who are not even in the job now. Football is that kind of industry. When you're assessing the job here you have to get somebody who has the longevity and the experience over a long time to manage this club. That is why David [Moyes] was above everyone else. I hope he can survive long term. It's the one club he could do that at. We've shown great loyalty to our managers.

"Football is a harsher environment these days, just look at the number of sackings, with Mancini being probably the biggest example. The owners are not English anymore, they are American, Russian, Middle Eastern, and therefore remote to an extent. It's a different culture. Agents are another big change since I came into the game, and I'm not sure for the better. I used to talk to parents, that was part of the job if you had identified a promising youngster. I don't even know any parents anymore. I just deal with agents all the time."

What makes Sir Alex tick? I went in search of dozens who met him, crossed swords with him, knew him the best...

The long-standing chairman of the PFA, Gordon Taylor, tells me, "He would be my top spot in the pantheon of the greatest managers such as Sir Matt, Jock Stein, Bill Shankly, Brian Clough, Bobby Robson, Kenny Dalglish, Pep Guardiola. And a great union man as an apprentice, as a young man in Glasgow, as a player and as a manager." Taylor was hugely complimentary of Sir Alex as a man as well as a manager despite their run-ins in the past, on one occasion bordering on the violent. Taylor bears no grudges, and he hopes that Ferguson feels the same. Gordon continues, "I have to say I am a big admirer of Alex Ferguson and the job he's done both at Manchester United and Aberdeen. He is the most successful manager ever to come to England from Scotland. I was particularly impressed by his youth policy at Old Trafford; the perfect model for every other big club in the game. Even though the club has such mammoth resources they have periodically developed their own home-produced players when they could have bought in players from any part of the world. It certainly paid off with the Neville brothers, Beckham, Butt, Scholes and Giggs, with other top-quality youngsters coming through now.

"Alex is a very strong-minded individual. He was not only captain of his ship, but he also wanted to know everything that was going on in his ship – that's the way he has always run things. Alex always remembers his grass roots from Glasgow, his trade union background. He has been a big supporter of the Scottish PFA and he supports us whenever we ask him. He was our guest of honour at one of our awards dinners. Of course, being the personalities that we are, we are both very passionate about the game. We have had our clashes and agreed to disagree at times. Yes, we have been close to coming to blows, but we haven't quite!"

Ferguson and Taylor clashed during England's match against Switzerland at Wembley in November 1995. Two of the most prominent figures in football in their day locked in an eyeball-to-eyeball slanging match in a row over the manager's video which featured Ferguson criticising Alan Shearer for being greedy in his wage demands by joining Blackburn rather than United. Taylor called for Fergie to face a disrepute charge after reading about the video in the press. When the two met at Wembley shortly afterwards tempers boiled over. Taylor waited until the area by Wembley's banqueting hall was quiet before approaching Ferguson. But the argument, which took place at the start of the second half, was witnessed by at least one FA official. The two men had hoped their clash would remain private, but the fact that it leaked out was embarrassing for both of them.

Fergie had launched the video in Manchester and travelled to London for promotional work. Taylor, asked to comment on the video, said that Paul McGrath had been found guilty of bringing the game into disrepute after remarks about Ferguson in his book, and so Ferguson should be brought to task for making adverse comments about Shearer. Taylor spotted Ferguson at Wembley and decided to explain his views. Ferguson's language was typically forceful, and the situation developed into an amazing scene. Ferguson never commented on the outburst.

Taylor says, "Grudges? I hope not. We have clashed at times. We had our disagreements over work permits for certain players and over disciplinary matters. He is a very strong supporter of his players, and at times there have been some very delicate issues to sort out. We had our differences when Alex was the subject of criticism when Paul McGrath left the club. There was a problem with Norman Whiteside and Paul McGrath having a worrying clique at the club, and Bryan Robson. Alex felt that both Norman and McGrath ought to consider retirement because of their injuries. That was like a cold bath to McGrath as he wanted to carry on. But there were deep concerns about his fitness and whether he was looking after himself properly." That is soccer-speak for a drinking problem. Taylor, however, was being diplomatic.

He went on, "A decision was taken by Paul that he didn't want to retire and take a settlement but wanted the opportunity to join another club and, of course, he went on to continue his career with Aston Villa and the Republic of Ireland. It worked out well for Paul in the end, but he was upset about leaving Manchester. He made some critical remarks and Alex was naturally concerned about them and very sensitive about them. A complaint was lodged with the Football Association. Paul was found guilty and fined a considerable amount of money."

But the issue of the Ferguson video made the sparks fly at Wembley, "Alex made references on the video to players who had left the club, like Paul Ince and Andrei Kanchelskis, and also commented about why Shearer didn't go to the club. I felt there were sensitive circumstances about why players had left the club and that he ought to be careful about remarks concerning players no longer at the club. How did my remarks about Alex go down? They went down like a sack of King Edwards! The result was the altercation at Wembley where I had to stand my ground. It didn't come to blows. Nearly, but not quite!"

Whatever has occurred in the past, Taylor's admiration for Ferguson is undiminished. "Our relationship is fine. I would like to think there is mutual respect for each other. I've been particularly impressed by the way he looks after players who have fallen on hard times. David Busst [The Coventry defender who suffered an horrific injury against Manchester United in 1996] is a case in point. He is always willing to bring down his team for a testimonial for a worthy cause, despite a congested fixture list – one aspect of the man that isn't lauded. That is a sign of the bloke's charity."

Few people in the game are equipped to compare Sir Alex with Sir Matt. The Law Man is one of the few. He played in Sir Matt's European Cup-winning team as part of that legendary Holy Trinity – Law, Charlton, Best – and is one of Ferguson's long-standing friends. Denis Law told me, "Yes, I have known Alex for a long, long time, going back to the sixties when he was still playing in Scotland. I thought then that here was a guy who craved success and would get what he wanted because he knew what he wanted to achieve in life. Celtic and Rangers dominated Scottish football then as they do now and yet he took Aberdeen to the very top, and that in itself – bearing in mind the strength of both Celtic and Rangers – was a great achievement and gave you the feeling he could do it elsewhere. He took Aberdeen to the championship and triumphs in Europe, including winning the Cup Winners' Cup, but coming down to England is always a difficult job and he did have a couple of years when it didn't go particularly well for him but then everything slotted into place.

"His achievements have been truly fantastic. Certainly I would put Alex right up there alongside the great managers of all time, like Shanks, Busby and Jock Stein, particularly for what Jock achieved in Scottish football as well. Alex has been very much like Sir Matt in the way that he has brought the youth through at Old Trafford. Not only have they emerged in the United first team, they have become permanent fixtures. Not only that, they have progressed to the international team and become a permanent fixture there, too. With Alex's experience in the transfer market in buying the right players, coupled with the youth structure that has become a formidable combination, really, you can't do much better than that. Alex has great stature in the game and quite rightly so, and it is important that he has also chosen the right backroom staff, very much in the style of Sir Matt, Shanks and Jock Stein. Behind the scenes he has got everyone rooting for the club. He has built a family atmosphere and you need that to pull through defeats and cope with the pressures."

They haven't even had a disagreement, "Alex could be under a great deal of pressure and sometimes you cannot blame him for the way he felt. He was under scrutiny all the time and it must get to him at times. He is a different character to Sir Matt, and we've all heard that he can be a touch abrasive, but there were times when Sir Matt could blow a bit, although not as often as Alex!"

Mark Lawrenson didn't mince his words. "He's ruthless." Actually, not detrimental in a manager – in fact, he is paying Fergie a huge compliment. Lawrenson explained, "Even managers like genial Bob Paisley had a ruthless streak, and Fergie certainly has it. I don't know if that's a northern trait, but it's certainly something that the northern managers seem to possess. Alex Ferguson was a relative failure at Old Trafford in his first few years, but there is something that drives him on from inside that ensured he wasn't going to go out a failure. Having said that, he owes a big thank-you to the Manchester United board because they could easily have lost patience and said, 'Thanks very much, but no thanks.' Instead, they kept faith in him, and Alex went on to prove what a great manager he is. He's a winner. Nothing else interests him. The great acid test is that all the top players want to play for him.

"Sir Alex Ferguson could have become the first Scottish manager to coach the England national team. FA chief executive at the time of the first approach, Graham Kelly, was one of only a handful of people who knew the truth. Kelly told me how highly he and the FA rated Fergie, "I think his record of success in the game puts him right up there at the top. Comparisons are always very difficult, but it would be fair to say that it isn't getting any easier year by year and he has done it in the modern era. That ensures that he can stand comparison with the best of them. He possesses a passion for the game, and I always like somebody with passion for the game. His teams always play enterprising football, always want to score goals. He has got a ready smile... if you don't approach him at the final whistle! He has a good personality."

Many of the biggest names at the time were linked with the job when Terry Venables' position as England boss become untenable, but behind the scenes there was an early call to Old Trafford as kingmaker Jimmy Armfield was sounding out suitable candidates, including Glenn Hoddle. Kelly says, "We approached Manchester United when we were seeking a successor to Terry Venables. I went to Manchester to speak to Martin Edwards. I left it with him and a couple of weeks later he contacted me to inform me that he and his board would not countenance us speaking to Alex. It would have been interesting to have met Alex Ferguson and to have put him alongside Glenn Hoddle... an interesting situation. I know he would have relished coming down to Lancaster Gate for an interview, but it wasn't to be because he was padlocked at Manchester United. We spoke to Glenn alone."

The prospect of a Scot in charge of England! Even Hoddle's choice of right-hand man, John Gorman, caused controversy, one of the reasons being that he is a Scot! "Not an issue," argued Kelly. He explained, "We were involved in the process of choosing the best man for the job." Kelly has a wicked, dry sense of humour and has spoken to Alex many times since. Kelly says, "Do we mention it? Probably every time I see him! Alex got himself a new contract out of it – he owes me a drink for that. I would say we have quite a tie. The sad thing is that I don't drink. I'm sure I can find some way he can show his appreciation for all I've done for him! In fact, I have even picked up the tab for one of his managers' lunches. There was Alex, Howard Wilkinson and a few others at a meeting at the Alderley Edge Hotel where Jimmy Armfield and myself planned to attend in the afternoon. We couldn't make it for lunch, so we had to make do with tea and biscuits instead but I decided to pick up the bill for the managers, and only realised how much of a bad move it was to make the grandiose gesture when I saw the bill – they don't stint themselves these guys. That's another one he owes me – with no prospect of collecting on any of them."

Paul Dickov got one of the most bizarre 'bollockings' from Sir Alex. The former Manchester City and Arsenal striker tells me, "When I got my first managerial job at Oldham, I got a call from Sir Alex. He asked me, 'Why are you not calling me, and using me like all the rest of them?' I was a bit surprised by the call, but he told me that so many young managers starting to lean on him for advice which he is more than willing to give, but as this was my first job he gave me a bollocking as he wanted to know why I hadn't contacted him for advice!"

Peter Reid has an unusual insight into arguably one of the most cherished goals Eric Cantona ever scored for United, certainly one of the Frenchman's best-loved moments – nonchalantly lobbing the keeper with an outrageous chip and slowly turning, collar up, to bask in the cheers of an amazed Old Trafford faithful. United were already 4–0 to the good against the Black Cats. It was tough for the then Sunderland manager Peter Reid, so painful he wanted to look away. After the game, he was cheered by the post-match press conference when the United manager did something quite unexpected. Reid tells me, "When I was manager of Sunderland, that Eric Cantona chip meant we were beaten 5–0 by United, and as you can imagine it was a pretty deflating experience. But at his press conference, Ferguson said afterwards that his side were that good on the day that they would have beaten any team in the world. I thought to myself, 'Well, he's protecting me by saying how great Manchester United were, and that took away from the focus on just how poor Sunderland were on the day.' He had no idea that I was there, listening to him at his press conference. I thought that was a nice touch. I've always got on well with Fergie, always enjoyed his company and a glass of wine after a game when we were managers. I know he has a reputation that he can be brisk with people at times, but that's the nature of the guy, he is competitive in everything he does. And when he is sometimes aggressive with people it shows me how much a winner he wants to be and how much he will stand up for his team and his players. He has nothing else on his mind other than winning. That speaks volumes about the man.

"He didn't have it easy to start with at United, but when under pressure he showed what skills he has at decision making and management. He built all-round teams and had exceptional players like Keane, Scholes, Beckham, Giggs and had four or five other top youngsters coming through." Reid had more than just a good working relationship with Sir Alex, he considers him one of his friends, "People forget that I go back with Sir Alex a long way, first when I was a player at Manchester City and then when I was manager at Sunderland. When I was at City as player-manager, Sir Alex arrived at Old Trafford and he had some tough times in the first few years. What I admire most about Sir Alex is the way he dug in when the going was tough, and when he was getting a wee bit of flack. What impressed me was the way he took tough decisions, and looking back, none tougher than when he opted to leave out Jim Leighton in the FA Cup final replay and bring in Les Sealey. It's not something often remembered or talked about much, but it was a big deal at the time, and showed how determined Fergie was and prepared to make difficult decisions."

In the replay Lee Martin scored the only goal as Sealey kept out Palace. Ferguson's bold decision diverted two lives in different directions as well as changing the course of United history. Fergie's assistant at the time Archie Knox was reporting as saying, "Before that Forest game I know the directors said they understood what Alex was doing and they would stand by him. Obviously you wouldn't have wanted to test that backing... but people forget that in our first full season at Old Trafford the club finished second. Then Alex realised he had to move on established performers and introduce younger players from through the ranks. He wanted a latter-day Busby Babes. And he achieved that. It was really tough going, though, until he had shaped the team with signings and young guys, as he wanted. It wasn't until the early 1990s that all came together with Ryan Giggs, Paul Scholes, David Beckham and Nicky Butt establishing themselves."

Two of Sir Alex's closest confidantes in the media at the time were Joe Melling and Bob Cass of the *Mail on Sunday*, and it was Peter Reid's association with the same journalists that brought him closer to the United manager, as they would invariably sit down for interviews together, over lingering lunches. Peter tells me, "We would have some very lively lunches back in those days especially with those couple of journalists we both trusted and enjoyed their company. But it was a vastly different era back then, too. You had a vastly different sort of relationship with those in the media you trusted. A relationship between the press and managers that doesn't exist these days. So I got to know Alex well and to this day we still pick up the phone to each other for a chat, and it hasn't been easy for him during the period when he was getting over his health issues."

Dennis Tueart was the first to spot Fergie at Old Trafford, and it was long before he became manager. The City legend tells me, "Manchester United had opened their new executive boxes and lounge as Alex was visiting as the Aberdeen manager, and no one took any notice of him at that time. No one had a clue who he was. I invited him to join us in our box right behind the Directors Box."

Dennis lives a couple of miles from Fergie these days and recalls bumping into him at Altrincham. He tells me, "It was the opening of a new conference facility at the club and David Gill knew the vice-chairman there and brought Fergie down for the official opening. I was also there as a guest and had the chance to chat with Fergie for three or four minutes. The guy is a mentor for just about everyone in the game, there is so much you can learn from him, and I certainly did reading his book."

Harry Redknapp came across Sir Alex many times enjoying that famous bottle of red after matches. Harry told me, "For sure, Sir Alex was simply amazing, amazing, a truly great manager, one of the best of all time. I know everyone leaps to the conclusion he was the greatest, and you can see why they reach that conclusion with the incredible years at Old Trafford and indeed Aberdeen. But I would say it is really hard to say who was the greatest manager of all time when you look at what Brian Clough achieved as well. Cloughie was also truly amazing and for me a manager is often as good as his players, and Brian Clough didn't necessarily have great players to win two European Cups. Certainly I would put Sir Alex in my all-time top three, but Sir Alex did have great players at United, and if you have good players you have a good chance as a manager; it's a much easier job, I can tell you. But it can be an impossible job if you haven't got good players.

"It doesn't matter if you are Jurgen Klopp or Pep Guardiola, put them into a Sheffield United or a Burnley and they are not going to suddenly finish in the top six. People labelled Scott Parker a genius for getting Fulham into the Premier League, and let's face it, you might call him a genius because he was pretty fortunate to get a relatively average, at times, struggling team, up through the play-offs. Same at West Brom, with Slaven Bilic. But they find out how tough it is in the Premier League – if they haven't got the quality of player. To be fair to Sir Alex, he was a great judge of a player, but equally United had the money to bring in the very best, irrespective of the price, as they paid record fees for Rio Ferdinand, and went out and bought players of the calibre of Jaap Stam, Wayne Rooney and many others, as well as having the benefit of six kids coming through the youth team who were all superb. But I have always had the greatest respect for Sir Alex's achievements, and they cannot be undervalued, as I said, he had an amazing career.

"I have always got on with Sir Alex, and we also shared a big interest in racing as well as football. He still to this day has some nice horses, and he loves the races. I still see him whenever I am doing TV work, but I wouldn't say we are close or mix socially, but I always enjoyed that glass of red with him after matches."

Alan Brazil also shares a love of horse racing with Sir Alex and they would get together if they bumped into each other at the Cheltenham Festival. He recalls something very unusual when he was a star striker for Ipswich Town under the tutelage of Sir Bobby Robson, taking the European scene by storm. Alan tells me, "There I was sitting on the Ipswich Town team bus, and I think we were off to play in a pre-season tournament. All of a sudden, Alex Ferguson climbs aboard the bus, and he nods and smiles at me and the other players, as he sits next to our manager Bobby Robson. I found out what he was up to and it was pretty clever. He was clearly intrigued by the unusual style of the Ipswich town team at that time, where we had Eric Gates floating in that no. 10 role off the front players, creating too many problems for opponents the way he would find space in the 'hole', something quite unusual at the time plus the fluidity of players like Arnold Muhren, dictating play starting from a wide position, linking with Frans Thijssen, and the way George Burley overlapped. Fergie was fascinated by this and wanted to find out how the dynamic worked. Low and behold, would you believe it, we were drawn against Aberdeen in a European tie, and they had some wonderful players at that time like Willie Miller, Alec McLeish and Gordon Strachan, and we were given the run around at Pittodrie in a real ding-dong of a game, and they ran out winners over the two legs. When you look back, it was obvious that Fergie had picked up the way Bobby Robson's team played when he was a guest of our manager at that pre-season tournament. How much did he learn? Well, I'd imagine enough to manage to knock us out with his team!"

Brazil believes Sir Alex would not find managing in the modern era very palatable, "Sir Alex is still enjoying his football in retirement, but I am sure he is also glad he left when he did. We all know about and hear about the tales of the 'hairdryer' treatment and the 'in your face' methods he used. But the players now are a completely different breed. They would not stand for any of it, and tell him, that if he has a grievance, to go and speak to their agent. I am sure Sir Alex lies in bed at night thinking about that, and it would drive him to distraction."

Alan recalls the Cheltenham Festival, having a wonderful time in his company. "I was with Ally McCoist who joins me on *TalkSPORT*, and Sir Alex invited us into the owners'/ trainers' restaurant, and Ally knows him far better than I do, but we all ended up having a right giggle, a few glasses of wine and some lovely bubbly."

McCoist recalls how an aspiring young manager had a big influence on his life in his early teens. Ally attended Hunter Hill School in East Kilbride. He tells me, "Fergie and I go way back, must be to 1974 or 75 in fact. I was just a young kid, Fergie was manager at St. Mirren, yet he would pick me up from my school to take me to training with the kids, then he would drive me back home at night after training. He'd pick me up because he lived in the same town." Fergie would even give the fourteen-year-old Ally a couple of quid for a fish and chip supper. "By the time I made it to the first team, Fergie had left for Aberdeen." So what was the first thing Fergie would say to you when he came calling at your school around 4 o'clock. "He would say to me, 'You're late!'" and Ally cannot help to chuckle at the thought of it.

Terry Butcher has had numerous encounters with Sir Alex. He verifies Alan Brazil's account about the time Sir Bobby invited Sir Alex to the Ipswich training session. Butcher tells me, "Alex came in to watch us train. I don't think Bobby was too overconfident about it, but Bobby was always very accommodating and helpful. He helped Jose Mourinho and he loved helping other managers, so he let Alex came to our training session and extended him a very welcoming and warm reception. But it helped Alex beat us." Aberdeen went through 4–2 on aggregate after a 3–1 second leg victory at Pittodrie.

Butcher's battles with Fergie continued when the England international was recruited by Rangers and later when Terry became a manager himself, "We had a few skirmishes alright. I was up against his teams and we always got on well when we met up. I was Coventry manager when we drew with Manchester United 2–2 at Highfield Road around Christmas time. I was staying at the Crest Hotel in Coventry, just off the M6 and Sir Alex's team stayed at the same hotel. I knew they were having dinner at the hotel the night before our game, so I came down to say hello and we ended up having a chat together with Alex, Archie [Knox] and his coaching staff. I didn't wish him luck for the game the next day, of course, but we had a nice chat.

"Perhaps one of my proudest moments was being inducted into the Scottish Hall of Fame and making a speech with Sir Alex there. It was a great honour, made even better by his presence. I also bumped into him in Casablanca when the England team were playing there when Glenn Hoddle was the manager just before the

World Cup finals. I was working with BBC Radio 5 live and we were walking to the game having just got off our bus, and there was Alex also going to the game, I'm not sure why he was there, but I guess he was doing some TV work. He came and said a few words to us." Terry was spared experiencing the 'hairdryer' treatment, "The lads from England and Manchester United talked about it a lot, and he had that reputation going back when he was at Aberdeen. But when I managed I dished it out at times, but I don't think you can do that sort of thing these days."

Driving to Glasgow from Ipswich for the funeral of one of his uncles, the last person John Wark expected to see was Sir Alex. John tells me, "Sir Alex had known my uncle, I am sure they shared Rangers connections, but Alex turned up out of the blue." At Sir Bobby Robson's funeral John had a long chat with Sir Alex. "There were lots of famous people up in Newcastle for Sir Bobby's funeral, and all the big hitters there wanted to come over to chat to Sir Alex. But, to my surprise, he came over to me for a chat, reminiscing about Sir Bobby. He came across as a lovely man."

Danny Murphy was surprised by a chance meeting to experience the completely different side to the man. Murphy reveals, "I have nothing but respect and admiration for the man and his achievements, but initially I never actually came across him, even though I played against his United teams quite a few times when I was at Anfield. All I ever saw of him in those days was his stern face and I experienced that aura around him when it was all about his team, the game, and winning, especially against Liverpool with that fierce rivalry that existed. I never even got to shake his hand, there was always far too much going on for such pleasantries."

Then came that chance meeting. "Many years after I had left the game, I was attending a charity event in London and stayed overnight in a hotel. I walked out of the hotel to wait for a taxi, and bumped into none other than Sir Alex, and spent an amazing five minutes in his company. I saw a totally different character to the one I had become accustomed to, the one everyone sees, but here was a guy enjoying the conversation. He was laughing and joking, as he told me, 'You were a right pain in the backside scoring so many goals against us.' We talked a bit of football and he was very complimentary toward Stevie G and how much he wished he had him in his United teams, but of course he couldn't because Stevie was a Scouser! I saw a charming, smiling, joking, lighter side to the man, something I hadn't experienced before, and never thought that I would, as I had always thought of him as this fiery character which I had only seen in the arena of battle. I was even surprised he remembered me, and that was a big compliment in itself! He is an amazing man and he did an amazing job at that football club, he is most definitely one of the greatest managers we have ever seen."

This neatly led to the question of whether he is actually the greatest? "That is a difficult one, especially asking a Liverpool fan brought up on Shanks and Paisley, but yes he is right up there in that conversation about who is the greatest. It really depends on how you look at it, the criteria you use to gauge success. Sir Alex brought United back to where they should have been competing with the likes of Liverpool... So in conclusion you would have to say, yes, Fergie is one of the greatest, but whether he is the greatest, you would have to argue that Shankly and Paisley can have as much claim to that title as anyone."

David James' commitment to Liverpool meant he had little to do with Sir Alex. The ex-England keeper had the usual preconceived notions and only changed his mind after a chance meeting – in the toilet. "There was no love lost on my side for Sir Alex or for Manchester United. I didn't really care about them much from my side playing for Liverpool, apart from the fact that I respected him as an exceptional manager building exceptional teams. We passed each other many times in the tunnel before and after games, but we never spoke, and all I ever saw of him was a manager with his game face. Unexpectedly I was given a Christmas gift of Sir Alex's autobiography. You can imagine that I thought, 'What a cheek!' I had watched the guy on telly, and I was sure there was no way he would be giving too much, if anything, away in his autobiography. I was sure he wasn't going to tell me anything if I read it. So, I didn't read it.

"Many years went by and just a few years ago I was invited into the Royal Box at Wembley for an FA Cup Final. The strangest thing. I went to the toilet and bumped into Sir Alex. The strangest place for a first meeting, I know, but that's what happened. And what surprised me... he turned out to be one of the most decent blokes you would ever want to speak to. For so long being anti-Manchester United, I found myself warming to Sir Alex. During our chat I said to him, 'I really want to ask you a question? Out of curiosity back in 1999 when you released your autobiography, did you put everything in there?' He replied, 'Of course not!' Well, it proved a point to myself, that I was a good judge not to have wasted my time reading it. But I would hate to play poker against him. It was a rare chance meeting, as I don't expect to bump into him again, as I don't think he shops in Asda."

Despite being vindicated in shelving the book, David's respect for Sir Alex only increased with that meeting. "Despite our rivalry at the time, I always thought of him as exceptional, albeit, making that assessment remotely as I had never met him before, and having met him now,

I consider that view of him as exceptional being spot on. He showed me the personality side of his character, and it was easy to understand why he was 100 per cent able to guide his teams to so much success, changing coaches, changing star players, and still having that amount of success."

Colin Calderwood can't believe that Sir Alex brought his lunch to his table and cleared away his dishes. The former Scotland defender tells me, "When I first got a job at Northampton with their under-23s, after leaving Tottenham, I sent a letter to United asking whether I could pop in on Sir Alex and observe training. I got a phone call back from Sir Alex's PA inviting me up there on a Monday and I was told to, 'Get there early.' When I arrived I was instantly told to make my way upstairs as, 'The Boss knows you are coming.' He was working with an analyst ahead of a vital Champions League tie the next day, so I sat in the canteen, along with their goalkeeping coach Tony Coton and his assistant Mike Phelan. I was taken into his office for a chat and Sir Alex showed me the report on the opposition and he told me, 'Hang on while I get my boots,' as he took me to watch training, introducing me to everyone along the way from the laundry lady to the kit man, and after observing the training ahead of the big game, he showed me around, the gym, and the first team dressing rooms where they were all changing. A few I had played against in my time, Rio, Neville and Scholes, they all said hello, Ronaldo was there, who had no idea who I was, but I was with The Boss and that meant respect for whoever he brought in.

"He then took me to the canteen for lunch, and said, 'You're Scottish so you will want soup.' He went and got soup, then asked what I would like for main course, 'Fish?' He cleared away my soup bowl and went off and brought back fish and vegetables and cleared that away when I'd finished. He said, 'Sorry, I've got to go back to Old Trafford to see the press before our Champions League game, I'll tell the guys here to look after you, and you can watch the schoolboys.' It was just an unreal, unbelievable experience. To think Sir Alex got me my lunch and cleared it away for me! It was a humbling experience.

"It must have been nearly two years later and out of the blue as I was leaving the house to go off before our game when I was working with Chris Hughton at Norwich, I got a phone call from Sir Alex. He wanted a chat and a general catch up. I was pulling my socks on, with the phone under my shoulder, thinking, 'I'm going to be late' as Sir Alex was happily chatting away, I thought he'd never go! I was a young Scottish coach and he was only too happy to help me, but I know I wasn't the only one, he enjoyed helping many others. He was always so hospitable and respectful. One day I picked up a paper and Sir Alex had given me a mention. It was ahead of the England–Scotland game in Euro '96 as he mentioned I had been at Tottenham with Teddy Sheringham, and he was talking about Scottish centre backs like Colin Hendry who would be marking him, I thought, 'Oh bloody hell, how nice of him.'"

Avram Grant, the manager who came the width of a post away from winning the Champions League in a penalty shoot-out, told me, "As a young guy, I was a guest of Sir Alex's at the training ground when he started out as coach of Manchester United. Then, my first game for Chelsea was against him, and my last game for Chelsea was against him, and also when I was at Portsmouth. I met him a few times, especially before games when he liked to come into the office. He's a great guy. Of course after games he would like a glass of red wine, and I gave him one of the finest from Israel from Golan, and he liked it."

Ken Bates once told me, "Alex Ferguson has my utmost admiration for his success, and it is his great attention to detail that impressed me the most. To become the greatest British manager of all time there has been some fierce competition, with Bill Shankly and Bob Paisley, but he has probably surpassed both of them – and he is still there. Matt Busby was a fantastic manager. He had flair and style and did it, 'Off the wall' in many respects. In comparison Ferguson is ruthlessly efficient, the most thorough professional in the game ever. I have never seen anybody in the game so dedicated, so professional, so thorough. He still had the team that everybody had to beat to win something. He has quite a sense of humour that is not obvious to a lot of people, and because of that we had our little banters from time to time. I loved to get him going, and I can say something totally outrageous to him and he will burst out laughing rather than take offence.

"When we lost to Manchester United in the FA Cup semi-final at Villa Park, I bumped into him immediately after the game and said, 'Who says crime doesn't pay?' At first there was a look of outrage and then he just burst out laughing. I have heard that when Alex Ferguson took over at Aberdeen one of his first tasks was to call together all of his scouts. So the story goes, he told them that he didn't want to discover that any kid who lived within a thirty-mile-mile radius of Pittodrie had signed for any other club, or he would beat the living daylights out of the scout responsible. The upshot was that he developed an exceedingly good youth team! Now, you've got to admire something like that. If it's true of course."

Ruud Gullit once told me, "He asked me to join him at the club's training ground whenever I wanted to. I saw him again at the World Cup and he told me he still wanted me to watch his team train. We have respect for each other as managers and coaches. It's okay to be enemies on the pitch, but we can respect each other's work."

Fergie admitted in his Old Trafford match-day programme notes that he regretted not signing Gullit as a player. Gullit says, "Yes, I remember that, and once again that shows that we have a lot of respect for each other. He was very strict. He knew exactly what he wanted and most importantly he knew how to transmit this to his players. This was perhaps his best quality."

Ferguson might be a superb communicator with his players but Gullit laughs loudly when he adds, "The problem is that I cannot understand him all the time – it's that accent!" Gullit enjoys Ferguson's company. "He is very comfortable, he is very funny. He talks a lot and I like to listen to him talk. He tells some wonderful stories about the game, and it is nice to hear someone of such vast experience imparting such knowledge. He has benefited from having the chance to be the coach of a club like Manchester United for a long time, and in an era when directors are not so patient and want immediate success. The club have not underestimated his abilities and understood those qualities and kept going with him until he brought the success they wanted. That is a lesson for many clubs to follow. Directors must have more patience... Rome was not built in one day!"

Sir Alex is a big supporter of the League Managers' Association and remains a valued member of their management committee. Due to his commitment to the LMA, many managers pay their respects to him. Peter Shilton had a spell as manager of Plymouth Argyle, and even though he didn't know Sir Alex personally, he sent him a message. Shilts tells me, "Manchester United had been pipped for the title in the last game of the season, I think it was a draw with West Ham, and I sent him a telegram saying,

'Better luck next time, I'm sure next year you will win it!' I didn't actually know him personally, although I had met him on golf days and charity events, and such things, but he was held in such high esteem, he had a presence, and you felt that presence from the second he walked into a room. He was an immense presence, a man who didn't suffer fools gladly, and I felt a common bond with him because of the way he liked good football, very much the way Cloughie and Taylor loved to play the game.

"It is always interesting when people ask me to compare managers or ask who would be my greatest manager of all time. So hard to come to the right conclusion. Take Cloughie, he won the European Cup twice, but didn't have anywhere near the sort of budget of Manchester United. Considering the size of Nottingham Forest compared to the mighty Manchester United; and Cloughie also was hugely successful at Derby County, then you have to put Cloughie's achievements into that sort of context. Fergie's career really took off, though, not by big money buys as such, although United could and still can afford the very best, but by the emergence of so many gifted youngsters all at the same time, such as Beckham, the Neville brothers and Nicky Butt all coming through the academy system. For me Eric Cantona was his best signing for United, albeit a bit of a gamble at first, it came off because he's the sort of character who could handle him."

Former Millwall goalkeeper Bryan King lives in Norway operating as a talent scout and has had many personal dealings with Fergie. On one of his multitude of overseas spying missions, Fergie travelled to Copenhagen just before the World Cup Finals to watch Denmark v. Norway. Ferguson was captured on a TV show knocking on the hotel door of Norway manager Egil Olsen after the game. Fergie looked a little surprised to see Egil's wife and daughter there when he entered the room. The Norwegian manager noticed Ferguson's bewilderment at seeing his family with him at such an important game.

Egil: "Don't you take your wife to matches?"

Ferguson: "Never... apart from the odd Cup Final."

Ferguson wasn't too pleased to be on Norwegian TV, particularly as a little later he was spotted by the TV camera hobnobbing with notorious soccer agent Rune Hauge and chatting over a cup of coffee with Ronny Johnsen as they discussed his injury problem. King told me, "I remember during Alex's early days at Manchester United when he came over to Norway on a scouting mission with his former chief scout Tony Collins, whom he inherited from Ron Atkinson. His mission was to run the rule over a young Norwegian player, Claus Eftevaag, and we all went to the under-18 international match between Norway and Sweden. Alex was very keen to see the player as he knew that Liverpool were also interested. He is extremely methodical and likes his scouting missions.

"We drove to Fredrikstad and saw the game but found ourselves plagued by journalists who had discovered that Alex was in town – and it was big news. After the game we were meant to have a chat with the boy, but we were engulfed by reporters wherever Alex went both inside and outside the ground. In no uncertain terms Alex informed one of the journalists and a photographer precisely where they could stick their pens and cameras... a place it would be difficult to remove them from! He was put under pressure but showed great restraint and diplomacy. He just dealt with a very irritating situation in a typically Scottish way. Just to cap his day we were stuck in traffic on the way back to Oslo for three and a half hours. Alex asked me if I knew a short cut. 'Yes,' I told him, 'if we had taken a boat!' He replied, 'Maybe we should.'"

King recommends players but Ferguson preferred to make a judgement based on personal viewing as well as watching videos and reports from his scouts. King said, "He first watched Henning Berg when he was seventeen and wanted to sign him when he saw the potential then but couldn't get a work permit for him. Whether he watches a youth team player or an established international, he has the same eye for it, looking for something out of it. He simply has such a great knowledge of the game. On a personal level I've probably been very lucky in my dealings with him – I've never got on the wrong side of him. Actually, I think he is a splendid chap. I've always found him to be the sort of bloke who will remember you."

John Barnwell, former Wolves manager, rang Fergie about the sixth annual League Managers' dinner and presentations at Sopwell House Hotel, St. Albans, in May 1998, where Arsene Wenger was Manager of the Year as Arsenal had just taken United's title. Fergie indicated he was attending, and Barnwell invited him to play in the golf tournament that preceded the dinner. Ferguson agreed, saying, "I've got to win something this season!"

Former England international Alan Hudson was run down on a zebra crossing and left with life threatening injuries. He was in recovery when he came into contact with Sir Alex in the offices of the then West Ham manager Harry Redknapp. Huddy tells me, "I was in and out of hospital in Whitechapel at the time and on a Saturday I would go to West Ham to see Harry and after the match go into his den where his guests would enjoy his cheap Bulgarian wine, which we'd laugh about, but it was always a great crack win, lose or draw. After this one match Sir Alex came in with his sidekick Steve McClaren and we were chatting away and Harry mentioned luck, and said, 'Look at Alan, how lucky was he?' talking about my great escape in Whitechapel Road. I pointed to Alex and said, 'I'm not as lucky as him!'

"Harry flinched as Alex replied, 'Too true, you'll get nowhere in this game without luck,' and told a story about a manager's office he went into after a match which had a sign behind his desk with the words, 'There's no such thing as luck.' Fergie turned to his sidekick on the way out and said, 'If he believes that, he's got no chance in the game,' and the manager hasn't been heard of since. He was a former Everton player under Howard Kendall in a championship winning team. Me and Alex got on famous on that day, like we had known each other for ever.

"A few weeks later I had to go to Old Trafford to see Bryan Robson, funnily enough when they were playing West Ham. I was with my son Allen, a mate called Paul McCormack and former jump jockey and pal Jimmy Duggan, who was second string to John Francome at Fred Winter's. We had two tickets which Jimmy and Allen were using because after seeing Robbo I was going to meet Sammy McIlroy in a pub nearby. In the stadium I spoke to the receptionist and said that I was here to see Bryan, so she rang him upstairs and he said to send us up. Along the way in the car I was telling the chaps about me and Alex at Upton Park and how well we get on. As we walked through the door and into the corridor leading to the elevator I said, 'Here's Alex now coming towards us,' and smiled ready to shake hands while noticing he had a face like thunder... He said, 'And where the f****** hell do you think you're going?' I said, 'I have a meeting with Robbo, Alex, upstairs,' and he said, 'The only place you're going is back out, so you can all f*** off out of here.'

"It was about 6.00pm and people were milling through, but he didn't give a f***, 'Yeah, you heard, f*** off out.' We went back through to see the reception and I asked her to call Bryan so we could set up another meet. She called him and Bryan said to put me on the phone, which she did. I told him what had happened, and he explained, 'He's just gone mad in a team meeting. Come back through, he'll be alright once he's settled down.' So we walked back through and I thought, 'If he comes through again there'll be murders.' I often wonder what would have really happened had he walked back through. I think I would have burst out laughing. In all fairness he was the only manager in those times I would not have argued with even though we did nothing wrong, as he was Mr Manchester United and that is something you cannot argue with.

"As for ranking him I think the only way to rate him would have been amongst the likes of Nicholson, Shankly, Waddington, Cullis, Greenwood and Mercer in our game but in the modern game he was the master, the best for building three different teams, all successful. He also was the best because he knew and bought the best players around from van Nistelrooy, to Cantona to Teddy [Sheringham], and then he turned Keane into an attacking midfield player. I used to watch him a lot under Clough, and made him the man who, like Bryan Robson was the pulse of the team. That's why I never questioned him throwing me out, in fact, I found it very amusing and showed he wasn't two-faced."

Sir Alex's help seems to be a very broad brush. Ramon Vega, a Swiss international centre-half, best known for his spell with Spurs, would seemingly have little link to the old United boss. He tells me, "I've met him at golf days, charity events and been in his private box at Old Trafford after a game. I've seen Sir Alex the man, rather than Sir Alex the coach, and this guy couldn't be more helpful, which is quite rare in this industry where mostly you are swimming with sharks. He can be very kind and prepared to open doors to help you not just in football but in the financial world where I now operate."

Cardiff City chairman Mehmet Dalman describes Sir Alex as, "A great man, a great manager, the greatest in fact." Dalman told me, "I have met him over the years in my role as investment banker and football club chairman. What struck me about him was that his enthusiasm for the game was very contagious. For example I met him after a Champions League game, I am sure it was Leverkusen, and it wasn't the greatest result, a draw, but when he came into the boardroom he was enthusiastic about the quality of Manchester United's football, and I can imagine that he would generate that level of enthusiasm around his team. He was a true manager in the sense that he managed everything to do with the club, as well as being a top man-manager of everybody around him. He was a one-man theatre, the passion he brings you will see nothing like it nowadays. I would say without doubt he was the greatest manager to grace the game in these islands, and there has been no one to compare with him since. When you consider that he rebuilt Manchester United three times in his managerial career at Old Trafford and every one of those three teams won the Premier League, his achievements are beyond compare."

Dalman appointed Solskjaer Cardiff manager and knew how much the decision revolved around the advice of Sir Alex. Despite having to sack Ole, Mehmet has no doubt that Sir Alex is the one the latest United manager consults the most. Dalman adds, "Our appointment of Ole had nothing to with any recommendation from Sir Alex. In fact, I took the initiative to bring Ole to Cardiff and later our owner Vincent Tan took the initiative when he met him and approved the appointment. Ole was managing in Norway at the time, with Aston Villa keen to take him but Sir Alex played a role for sure in helping Ole make the decision. I was not party to the discussion between Sir Alex and Ole at the time, but Ole told me that he would take to Sir Alex before coming to his decision. I also know that during his time as Cardiff manager, he kept in touch with him. throughout the period he was there. I have met Sir Alex from time to time at Old Trafford, and once again when Manchester United came to Cardiff, and I know that he was very supportive of Ole and us."

Dalman explains how Ole was thinking of United as his ultimate goal, "We had a clear understanding that if the call came from Manchester United he'd be off. That was made very clear, that he would be free to fulfil his wish to manage Manchester United. Of course eventually that call from Manchester United did come, as a caretaker manager at first, but there was no chance that he would turn them down. It is still too early to judge him. He is a young manager and there are a few about now, such as Steven Gerrard, Frank Lampard, Mikel Arteta, and Ole and all of them, you really do need to give them time, something that is so often in short supply in football management. But at a club as big as Manchester United it is totally unrealistic to expect so much from someone so inexperienced at this level, but I think they will give him that time."

Aberdeen born Stuart le Gassick is one of Sir Alex's closest friends and says it is, "A pleasure to contribute to a truly great man and loyal friend." He tells me, "I was introduced to Alex by his lawyer Les Dalgarno from Aberdeen as a potential investor in my real estate fund AIM and was asked to meet Alex at a game at Old Trafford. I was nervous due to his reputation and as soon as I walked through the door of his room he took the piss out of my suit and tie. This took the sting out of the meeting and the banter continued for twenty years." Through the

Scottish-English banter he became known as Sweaty Sock Wilmslow.

"I bought a country house in Somerset and Alex rang and said, 'I understand you have bought a nice house and my Scottish friends and I are going to come down and wreck it.' After much banter we decided to have an England v Scotland weekend for charity. We met prior to the weekend to go over final details and I told Alex that I had asked David Mellor to come and speak on behalf of the English to which Alex replied, 'If he comes I won't.' Evidently Alex had sued David in the past and he won but his costs outweighed his winnings. He saw that I looked mortified and said, 'Alright, I will come, I will shake his hand, but I won't kiss him.'"

Sir Alex threatened legal action against Mellor for something he said during his stint as a 606 presenter on BBC radio 5 live, to which Mellor told me he has no intention of discussing. There is no information about the proceedings as they were dealt with in 'correspondence.'

Stuart continued, "The weekend was arranged for 120 people over a Saturday and Sunday with clay pigeon shooting and archery followed by a Burns Night dinner in a marquee with Scottish dancing and singing from Fiona Kennedy and many funny speeches. This was followed by a Sunday of the competitions with a St. George's Day Lunch and entertainment by The Wurzels. The event raised over £100,000 for an autistic school in Aberdeen. The Scots had chartered a plane from Aberdeen to Bristol for the event. When Alex and Cathy arrived on the Saturday his opening words were, 'Should be a great weekend and we have Scotland and England playing games before the dinner and we can watch the games on TV having a couple of beers.'

"I said there was just one thing, I had been asked by the local football team if Alex would sign a football at the local farm shop. Of course I was verbally abused but Alex said, 'Come on, let us get it over with.' We got in my car with Brian Turner the celebrity chef who was supervising the weekend's culinary offerings. After photos in the farm shop I said, 'Just one more thing, can you sign a shirt for the local school?" A few more F's and we were off. The signing was due to be at a local pub. I was mortified when I got close as the road was closed due to the amount of people there. Alex said, 'What have you got me into?' and I said to Brian, 'Let's leave the car and go into the pub for a pint.' I asked Alex if he would like a pint. I think I got an affirmative.

"After fifteen minutes, TV and radio interviews over, he finally arrived at the bar. I expected the 'hairdryer' but he said, 'Do you see that old bloke with a walking stick at the bar? He played for Scotland.' He went and spoke to the chap who told him he had heard Alex might drop into the pub. After he came back to Brian and myself he pointed to a group of the blokes in the pub and said one played for Bristol Rovers in 1974. I thought that was bullshit but I went over and asked if he had ever played football. He said, 'Not seriously, I only played for Bristol Rovers from 1972 to 1975.' We left the pub and got into the car and I subsequently found out that our beer mugs were auctioned off. Alex £35, Brian £10, mine, F. all. I thought the drama was over but while quaffing our beers and watching the footy, the doorbell went and David Mellor was there asking if he could watch the game. He had to sit on a couch with Alex. This is still the most difficult time I have experienced.

"The weekend was brilliant and I can say Alex, for all his success, is a fabulous guy with a wonderful family and we, all his friends, want plenty of more special moments. Many years ago I was working in Manchester and played five-a-side football for a local Chinese restaurant. Alex Stepney also played and we would wager between us who would score the most goals and spend the winnings in a local pub. One Saturday evening at 5.30pm a few years ago my phone rang and it was Fergie after a game. He said, 'You told me you could play the game but you were f****** useless.' He was with Stepney.

"In my fund we agreed to buy the biggest shopping centre in Europe. It was in Budapest. The developer rang and asked if Alex would officially open it. I replied that as it was in the middle of the football season he wouldn't, but I said I would ask him anyway. Alex asked me to a Champions League game and to stay at his house. We would get up in the morning jump on a private jet and do the opening. This happened and on the jet on the way back he asked me where I was going. I said, 'Are you thick, we are on a jet to Manchester?' He said due to the fact that he is a superstar he will get the pilot to drop me off at Bristol. And did."

Popular TV presenter Eamonn Holmes started out with humble beginnings and recalls his first encounter with Sir Alex. "I had come over from Belfast at virtually the same time Fergie came from Aberdeen. I became friendly with Fergie when I was a sports reporter for BBC North-West based in Manchester. I hosted a programme with Denis Law. I'd go to the training ground at The Cliff. One day Fergie called me over, 'Oi, can I have a word with you?' My God, I was terrified and wondered what he might want. 'You BBC lot,' he started, which made me feel even more apprehensive at what might be coming, 'Every one of them are paid up members of the Liverpool supporters club, your producer Brian Barwick, Hansen, Lawrenson, Alan Green... and you, you are the only one who preaches The Red gospel.' I wasn't quite sure of that, but with Fergie it was simple, you were for him or against him, and he clearly saw me as being with him. At the time I was doing a general programme as well as sport, but everybody knew my allegiances as a United fan. He loved the idea that I was a genuine United supporter. From that moment I got on well with him and had a good relationship. He would phone to invite me to events; family get togethers, wedding anniversaries, significant birthdays."

Because of a remarkably close relationship that developed, Eamonn has a profusion of personal stories about the great man. "One day I was in London catching a flight to Belfast, and so too was Fergie. When he spotted me, he went over to the check-in and asked them to put us together in row four where he was sitting. We spent the journey chatting football. This must have been twenty years ago, maybe longer. When we got off the plane, he asked, 'Where are you going now?' I told him, 'Boss, I live round the corner.' But he wasn't having any of it, and instead of a taxi, he insisted on giving me a lift. A massive S-Class Mercedes pulled up outside the airport. My suitcase in the boot, him and me in the back, we pulled off. I couldn't ring Ruth to warn her – no mobiles back then! Three minutes later we pulled up outside the house, I knocked on the door, Ruth opens the door, a dish cloth over her shoulder, her hair up, and looking quite hassled.

"Ruth doesn't like doing two things at once. She was cooking spaghetti and something else, and totally immersed in that. She stood there, mouthed some words, and I realised she was saying, 'How much do you want?' She thought I had taken a taxi, didn't have enough cash, and the driver was stood there with me waiting to be paid! Ruth doesn't like surprises and boy was she surprised when Alex Ferguson walked in! 'Hi, Ruth,' I said. 'This is The Boss, Alex Ferguson.' All Ruth could say was, 'Oh my goodness.' I continued, 'I've invited The Boss in for tea.' Again no smart phones to take a snap, but I did have a digital camera, and asked Ruth, 'Where is that camera?' Ruth wasn't having it, 'Don't you dare embarrass yourself, by asking for a picture.' But sod the embarrassment, here was The Boss in my kitchen, I had to have a picture.

"This all happened on a Thursday and that Sunday we were playing Liverpool and I had invited some mates and family round to watch the game. I wanted them to see that Sir Alex had been in our kitchen. I ran down to the chemist with the camera, got the pictures and got them framed, nice big ones, 8 by 10, one in our kitchen, one outside our front door, to show them that Fergie had been here, and placed them prominently displayed in our hallway, so everyone could see them when they walked in. The day came, I was so excited, but when they came into the house, saw the pictures, they were adamant that I had had them mocked up, they told me, 'Fergie in your house on a Thursday before this big game, don't be ridiculous!'

"Over the years I have known Fergie, he has taken the trouble to know my family. He knows the boys' names. I was lucky enough to be invited to do the MC when his statue was unveiled at Old Trafford, and I took Jack with me, he was only about eleven or twelve. I am sure he didn't want to go, and Ruth didn't like the idea that I would have to take him out of school for the day, but I told him, it was a special occasion which he would remember for the rest of his life, and to be glad that he was there. After the unveiling we had a special lunch and Sir Alex caught my attention, 'Come, you two,' he said, 'you are sitting here on this table with me.' We were seated with Bobby Charlton, Lady Cathy and David Gill. Sir Alex made such a fuss of Jack, asking him who were his favourite players. There was no question that Lady Cathy was in charge, though. They had a fantastic relationship, she would say, 'Where are you going, you stupid old goat?' I called Sir Alex The Boss, but she was The Boss alright, and he was very much in awe of her."

Eamonn wanted to add this very important point in the book, "When you get to know the real Sir Alex, you realise that he is actually really 'normal'. Of course many take him one way, as he remembers if you have been good to him, and he remembers if you haven't. But for me he reminded me of my dad, he was always concerned about the welfare of others. I like to be like that as well. Knowing him as well as I do, you appreciate his incredible thoughtfulness and kindness, as well as his brain which is like a computer. He can tell you what happened to him in every game he played, who would pass the ball to whom, and what happened then. He would love to tell you every last detail. He has a crystal-clear recollection of every detail; I couldn't tell you what I did last week. He is very much a family man, and he has always included Ruth in everything that has involved me, and he says he even watches *Loose Women* and would have a clear recollection of the debate as he would say, 'Did you hear what she said the other day?' And he would talk about that for an hour.

"For his 70th birthday he invited Ruth and myself, and he had a couple of celebrations. One for the football people and then one for his family. We went to the one at the Hilton Hotel in Manchester and there were people there from his primary school days to the likes of Alistair Campbell, Mick Hucknall and Ian McShane. By the end of the night we were all up and singing, I'm holding Fergie's hand, Ruth is holding his other hand, I'm holding Mick Hucknall's hand, who was holding Ian McShane's hand. When you want a camera, you can never find one. I'm a fan and make no apologies for that. I was thinking, 'If only my brothers could see me now.' Everybody in our family are Reds.

"For my 50th birthday I didn't really want to do anything but somebody suggested Old Trafford, so we hired a lounge there. United were at Southampton that day and won something like 5–1. I sent an invite to Fergie, but hardly expected him to show up if his team were playing on the south coast. It was a black-tie event, but Fergie did turn up, having flown up from Southampton, got himself changed, and came along with Cathy and stayed for the entire night. Everybody there wanted a picture with him or an autograph and he obliged everyone. Underneath all this incredible success, there was an 'ordinariness.' something quite different to his image as a ruthless winning hard man, driven by the desire for success. Look, I know it all sounds a bit cringy because I consider him a friend, but that is my view of the man and my love affair with United from the first time I was lifted over the turnstiles at Old Trafford in 1972 to the surreal times knowing the club's greatest ever manager.

"One day we were chatting about Christmas cards and he rattled off my address and postcode. I said to him, 'You don't write all those cards yourself?' He replied, 'Yes I write them all.' I was staggered and said, 'I thought Lady Cathy wrote them.' He said, 'No, I do them and sign each one.'"

Usain Bolt was delighted to offer his personal assessment, "Sir Alex Ferguson is a legend, not only in football but across sport for his achievements as the Manchester United manager. He took the job in 1986, the same year I was born, and only retired in 2013. In his twenty-six years in charge, he won two Champions League titles and thirteen Premier League titles. What makes him stand out so much is that he was able to keep rebuilding the team to maintain the success. When I started following Manchester United it was in a team with Ruud Van Nistelrooy up front. By this time, he had already won the treble and the Class of 92 were recognised as world class players. The addition of the likes of Cristiano Ronaldo, Rio Ferdinand and Wayne Rooney helped keep the team at the top throughout my lifetime."

Usain was always received with open arms by Sir Alex, they talked like old friends whenever they met up, "Sir Alex always made me feel very welcome at Old Trafford. I am a passionate Manchester fan and got to spend time with the team at Carrington and on match days. It was clear that he commanded respect from the players and they knew he was The Boss. In recent times, Manchester United has struggled to achieve the same level of success as they had under Sir Alex which further goes to show how good a manager he was."

Former England cricket captain and Director of Cricket at Surrey Alec Stewart has drawn inspiration from Sir Alex, as he explained, "As a massive Chelsea fan, I'm not supposed to like him, but I do. In fact I've mirrored a lot of what I do in my current role on how he conducted himself professionally, from listening to him on TV and reading his books, especially the way he protected his young players. Without knowing him, he has influenced me in the decisions I make in my working environment. I've met him a couple of times at League Managers Associations and charity events and enjoyed listening to his speeches. He is such a very interesting person, and everyone has total respect for what he achieved in football. He is a special person, and everybody can learn from him, whether in sport or in business."

John Lyall was one of the most successful managers in English football in the 1970s and 80s, so when Sir Alex first came to England from Aberdeen, the Hammers boss was one of the first he consulted, a fact that Sir Alex went out of his way to recognise. Hammers fan Ray Winstone, iconic star of TV and screen, recalls how Sir Alex honoured the Hammers boss. Ray tells me, "I only met the great man on one occasion for a couple of minutes, it was at Upton Park. A night remembering John Lyall that Sir Alex had flown down for especially. He gave a speech about his friendship and the respect he had for John and showed himself to be a great and entertaining speaker." In 2006 Ron Greenwood and John Lyall, the East End club's greatest managers passed on, and West Ham had a special dinner, at The Boleyn in honour of them. The Club invited Sir Alex and his wife Cathy as guests of honour. Despite Manchester United playing a crucial match midweek, Sir Alex attended as he always considered John Lyall a true friend and a man of integrity.

Alastair Campbell tells me, "There are no limits to Sir Alex's competitiveness. When my kids were young he was at our house for dinner one evening. My daughter – though not a football fan – was determined to show him off so she came back with her friends and they all stood in the kitchen and gawped. He asked them all what team they supported. The first two said Manchester United. The third said Arsenal. He said, 'Do you know if you support Arsenal that you're not allowed to have holidays when you're older. Did you hear about that law?' The little girl looked shocked. 'Okay. Man United,' she said.

"I raised both my sons Rory and Calum as Burnley fans. Mascots aged four. Took them home and away. When Rory was about eight he started getting interested in 'other' clubs. We were at home in the Championship or League One on a Saturday, United away at Newcastle on the Sunday. Rory said, 'Dad, why don't we have a weekend away and go and see another game on the Sunday. Maybe meet up with your mate Brendan Foster?' 'You know how we hate Blackburn?' I said. 'You're not becoming a United fan are you?' He said, 'No, just be nice to see a big game.' I called Alex and asked if he could get us tickets. I said I was worried Rory was shifting so said, 'No special favours, ordinary tickets, I don't want him to enjoy it too much.'

"'OK leave it with me,' he said. We arrived Sunday, went to collect the tickets and there was a message to see him. He came up from the dressing room, ignored me, looked at Rory, said, 'Do you wanna meet the players?' Took the boys to the dressing room. Becks, Giggs, Schmeichel, Neville, Scholes etc. Rory in dreamland. Burnley have been his second club since!

"He is of course a very tough character and can be very demanding and very harsh on those he feels fall short. But there is a heart and humanity to him that stems from roots he has never forgotten, and values imbued by family and upbringing."